Designing And Drawing Animal Tattoos

How To Draw Animal Tattoos

Animal Tattoo

By : Gala Publication

Published By :

Gala Publication
© Copyright 2015 – Gala Publication

ISBN-13: **978-1522707196**
ISBN-10: **1522707190**

Table of Contents

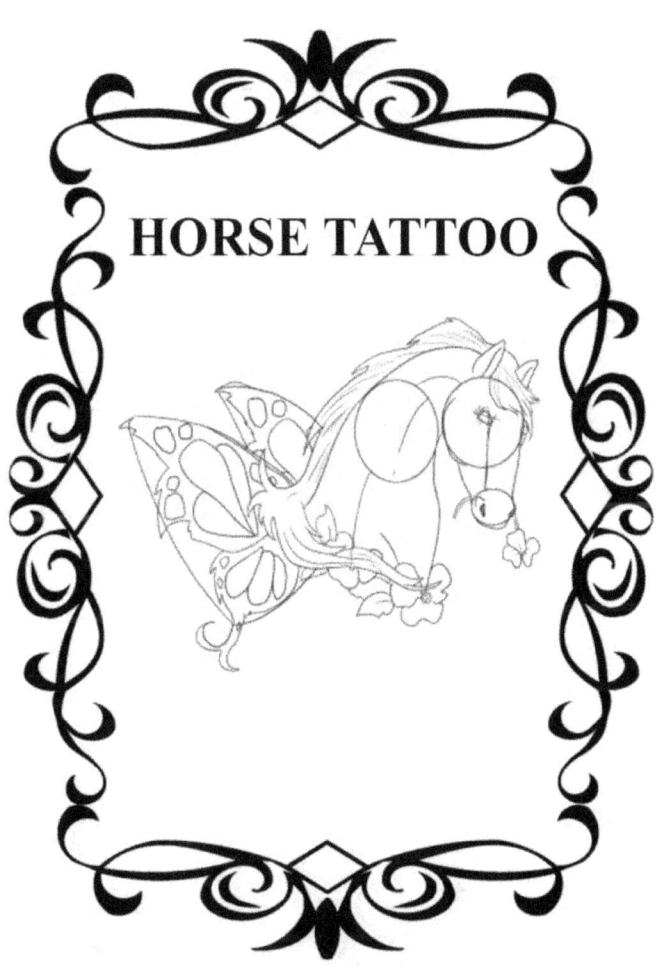

HORSE TATTOO

STEP 1

STEP 2

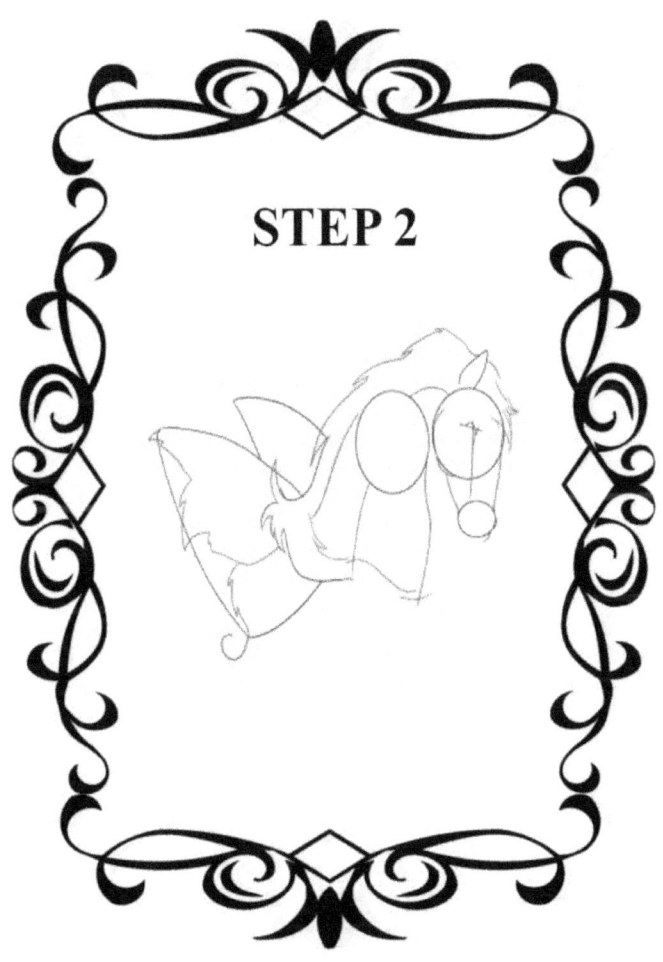

STEP 3

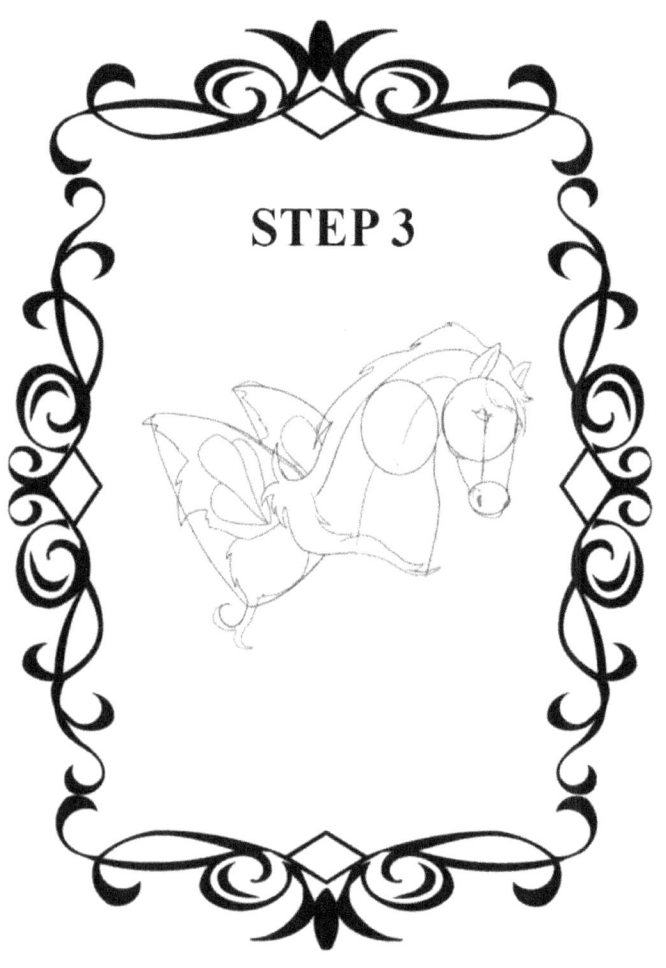

STEP 4

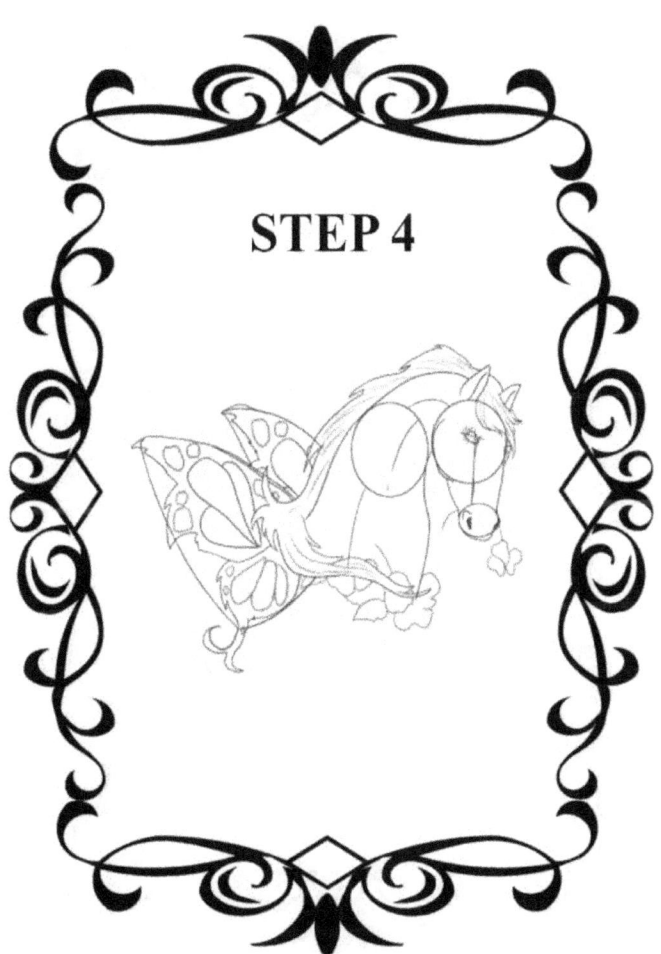

STEP 5

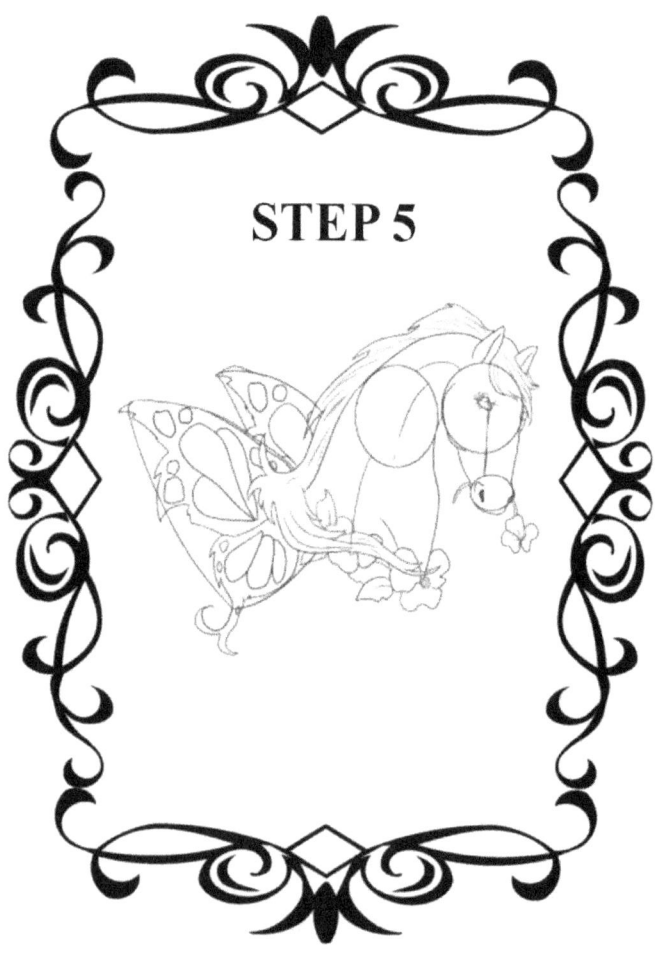

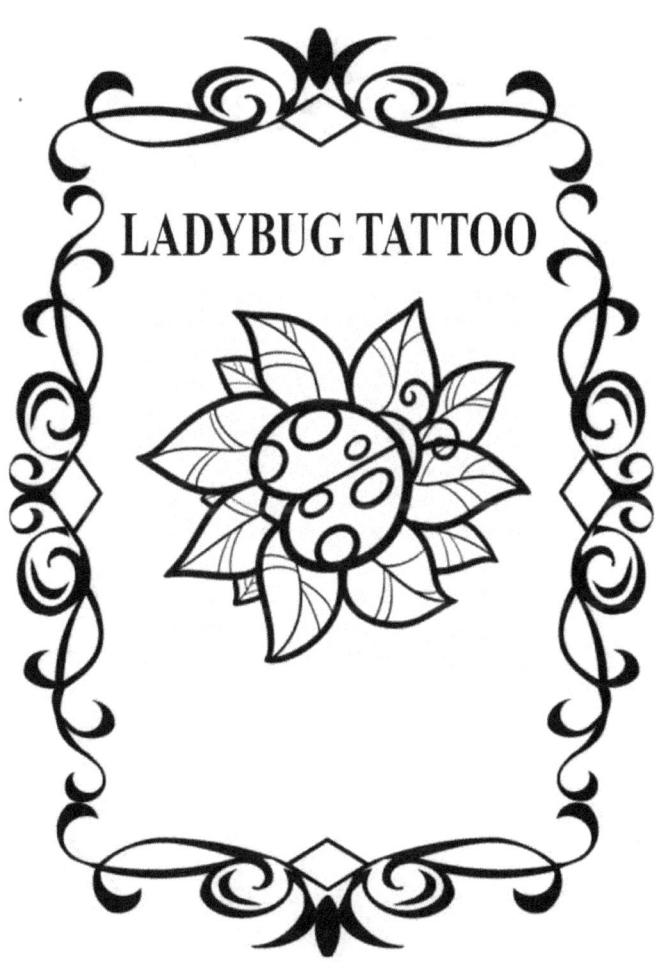

LADYBUG TATTOO

STEP 1

STEP 2

STEP 3

STEP 4

STEP 5

STEP 6

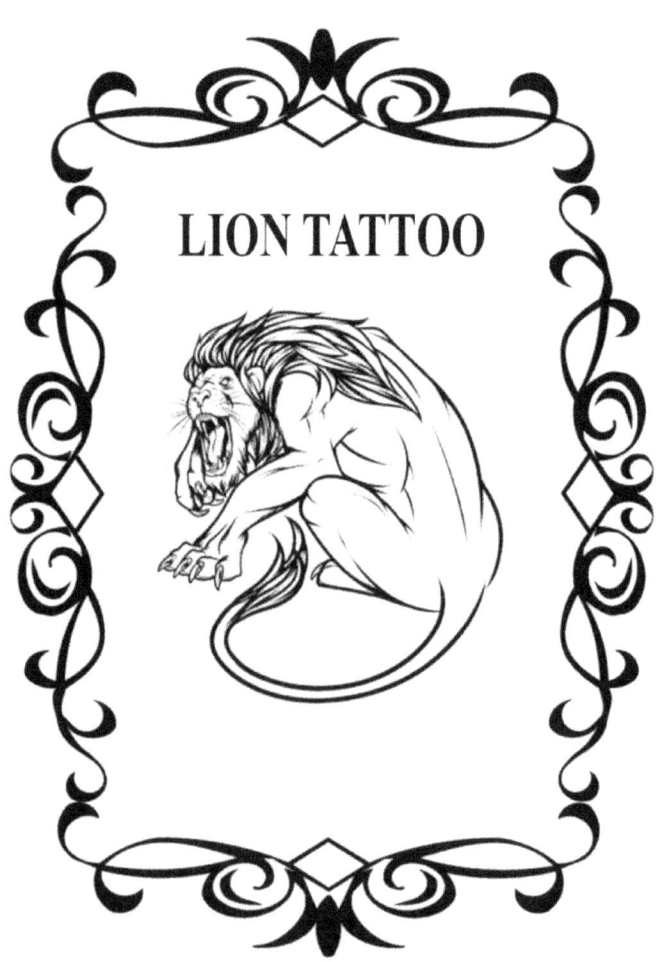

LION TATTOO

STEP 1

STEP 2

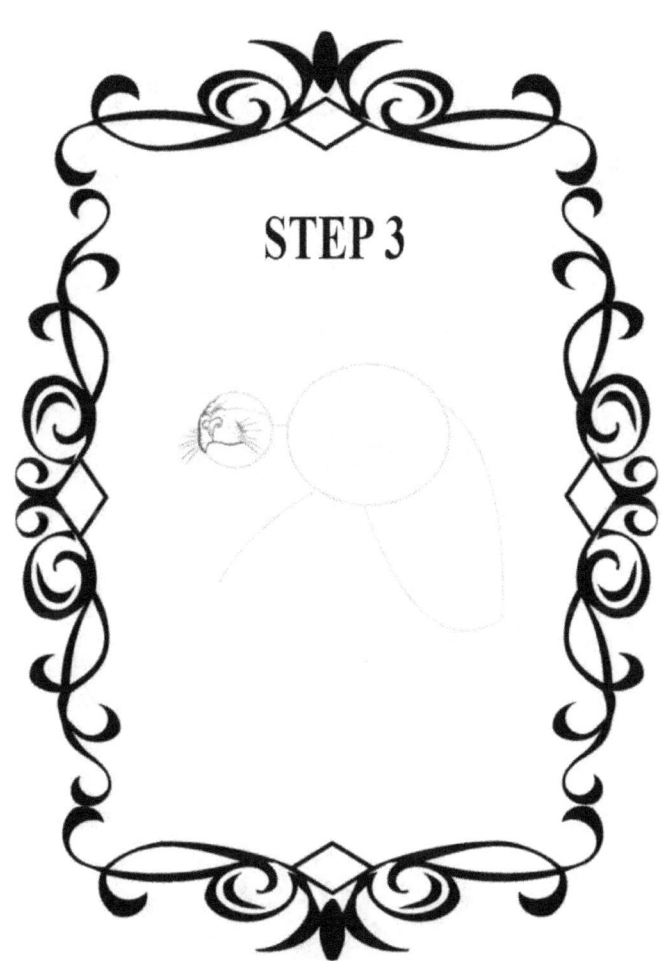

STEP 3

STEP 4

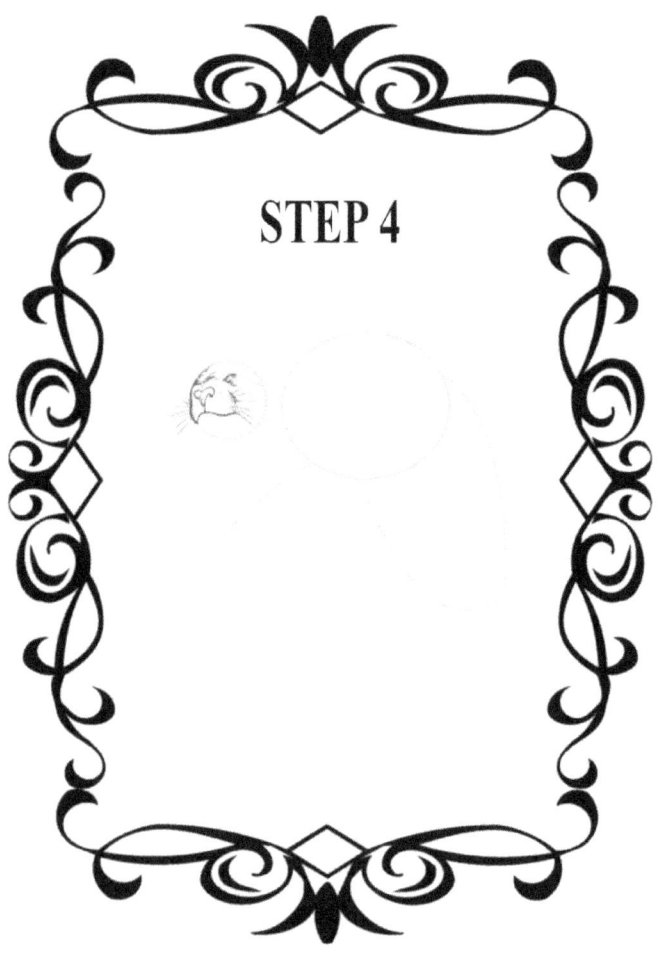

STEP 5

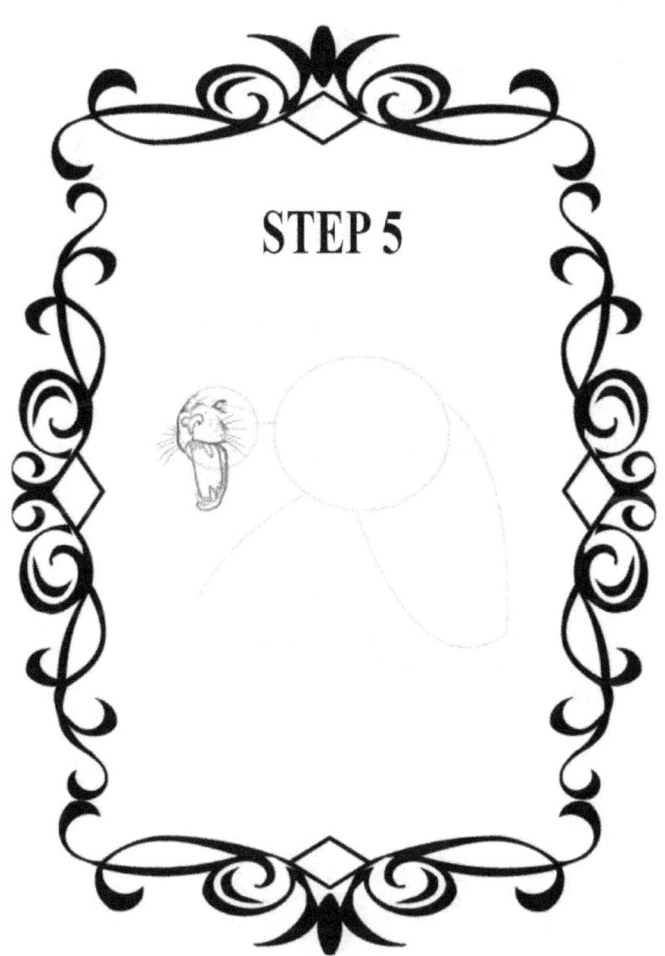

STEP 6

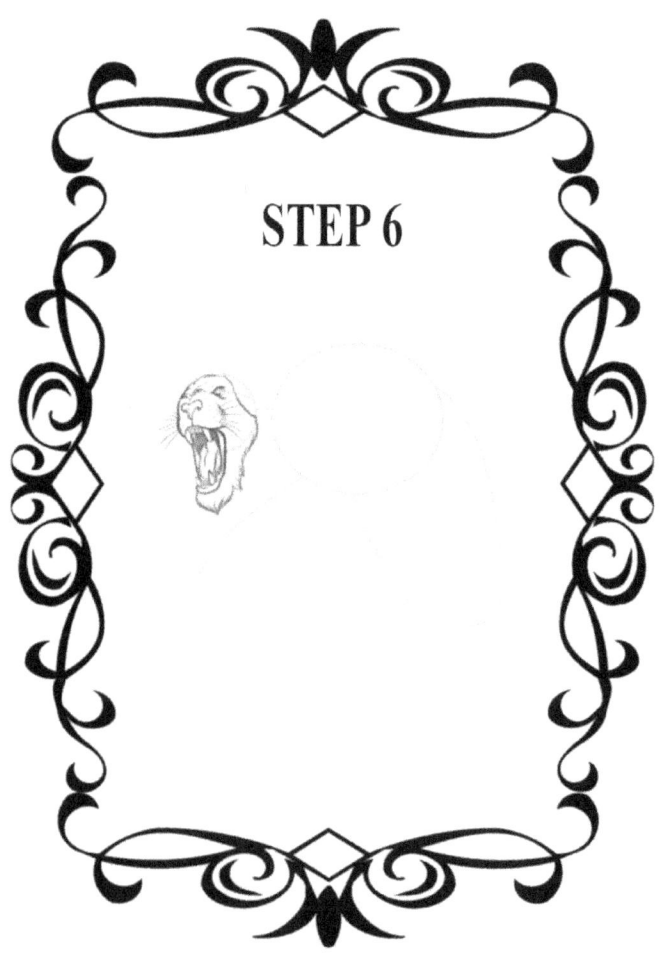

STEP 7

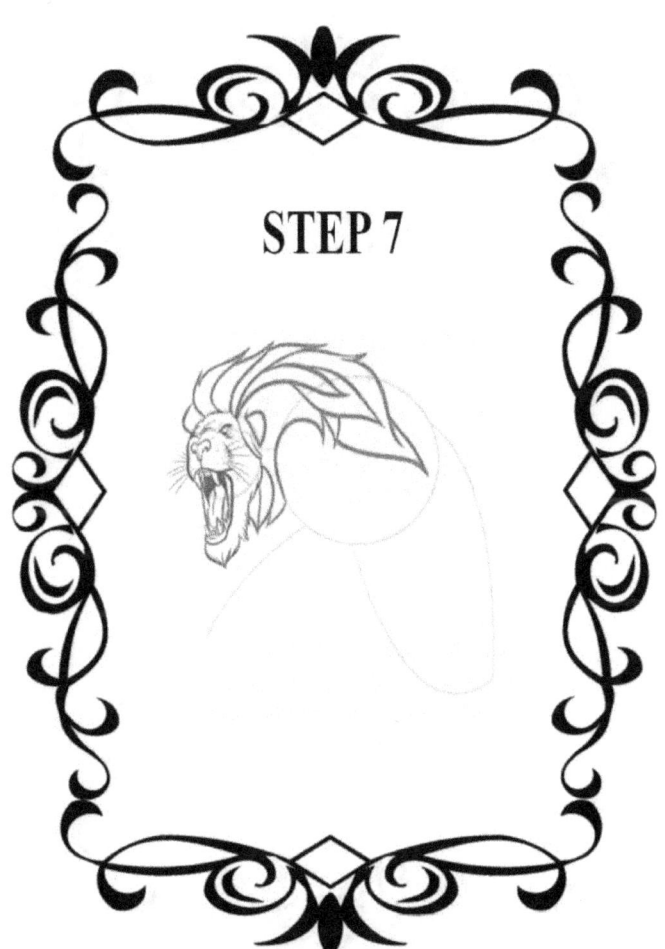

STEP 8

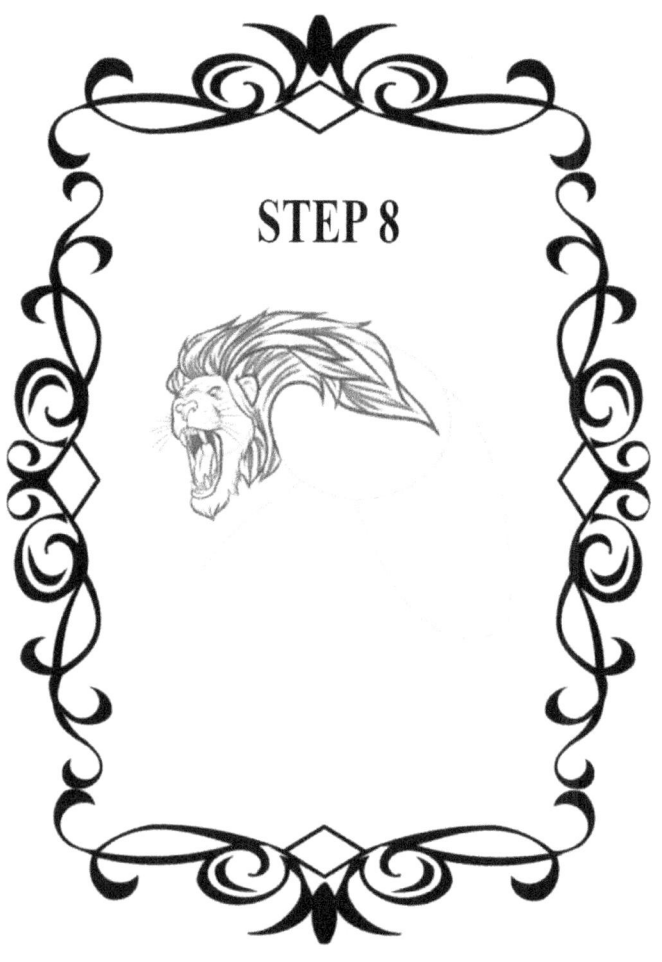

STEP 9

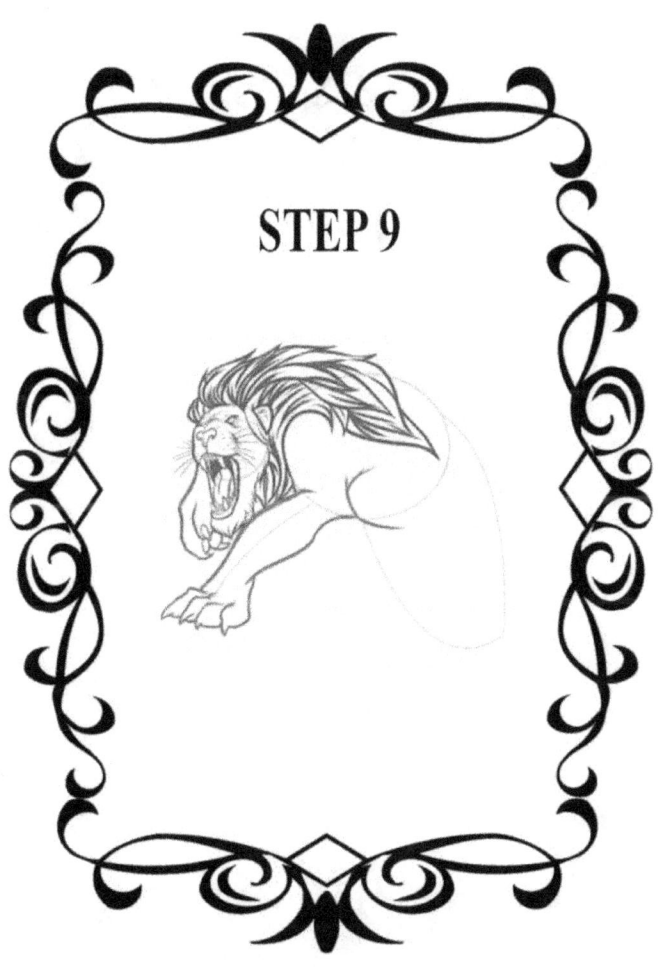

STEP 10

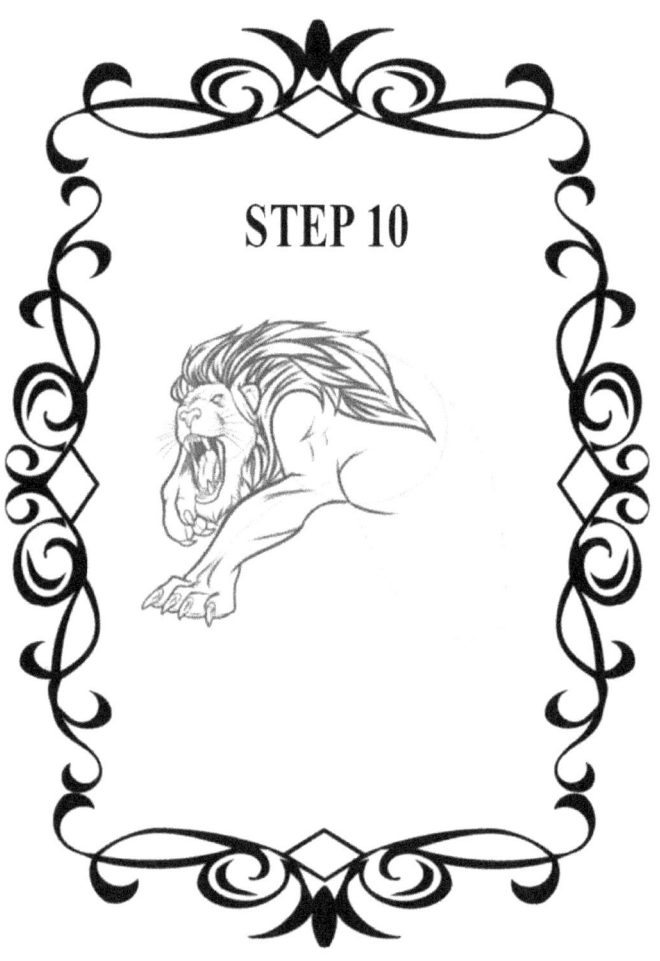

STEP 11

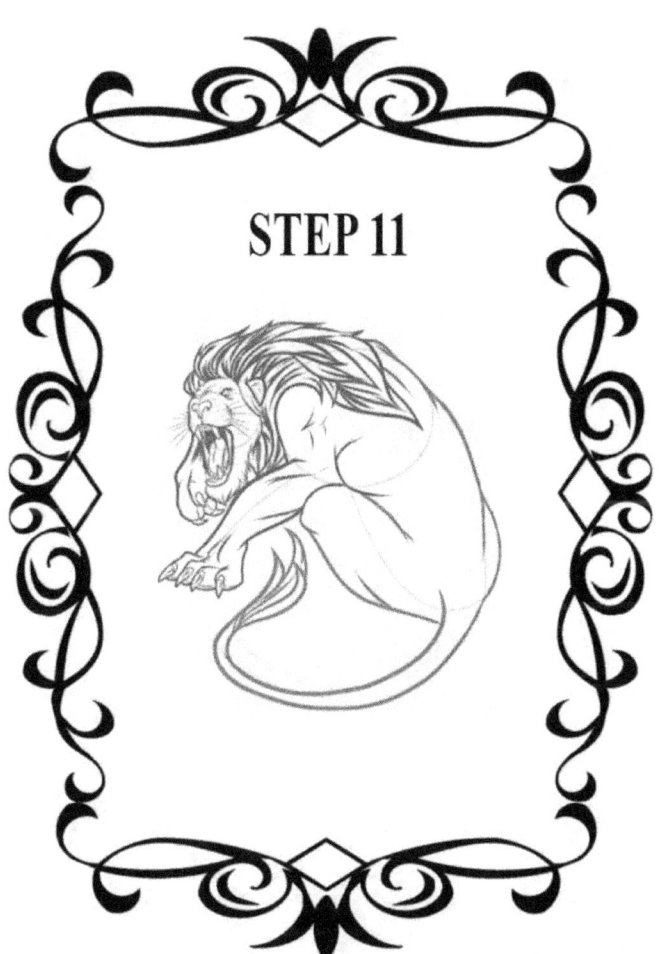

STEP 12

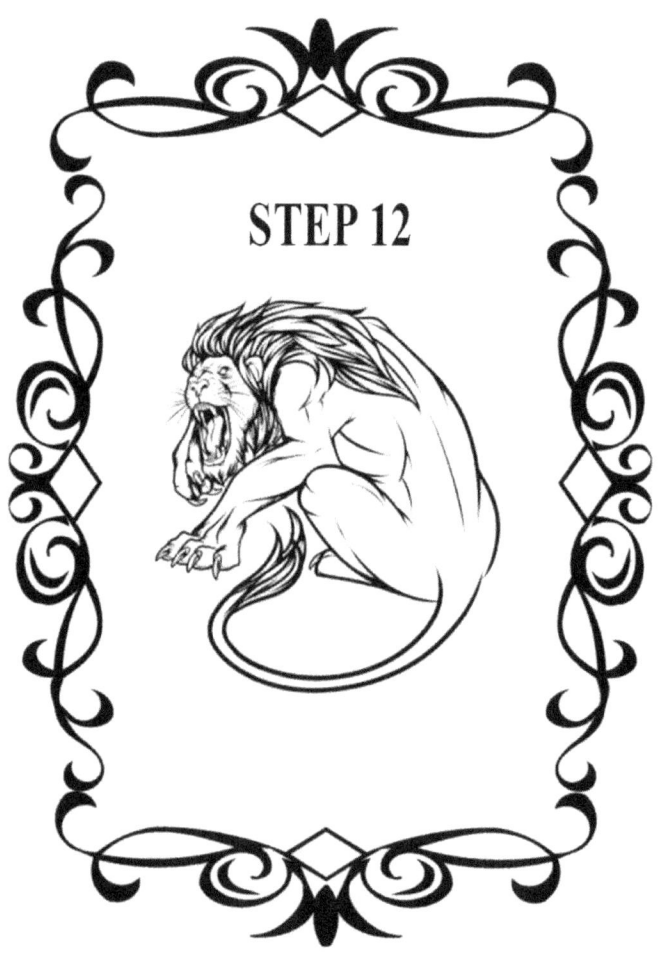

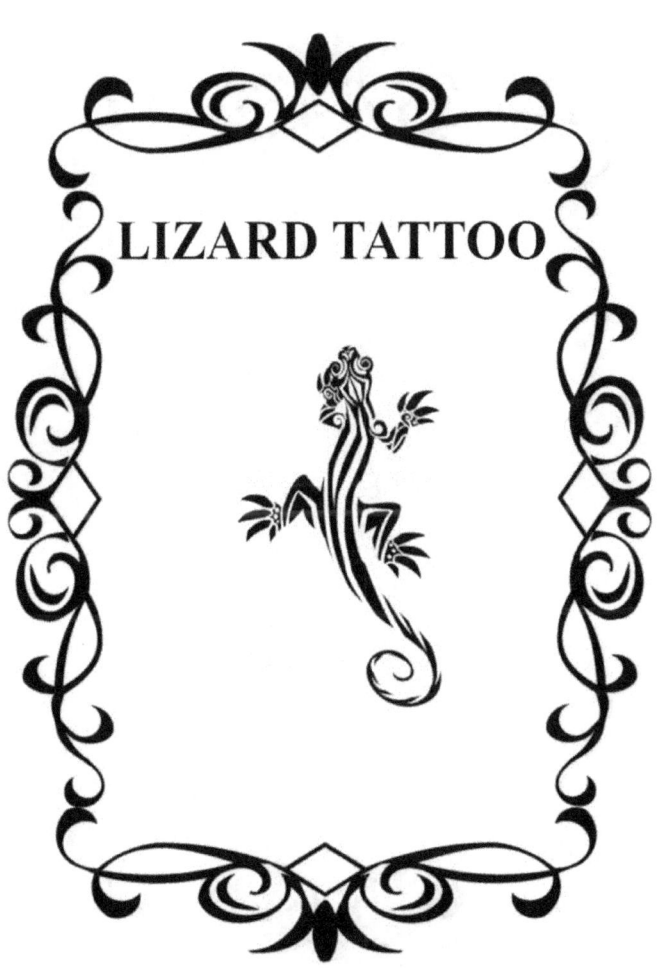

LIZARD TATTOO

STEP 1

STEP 2

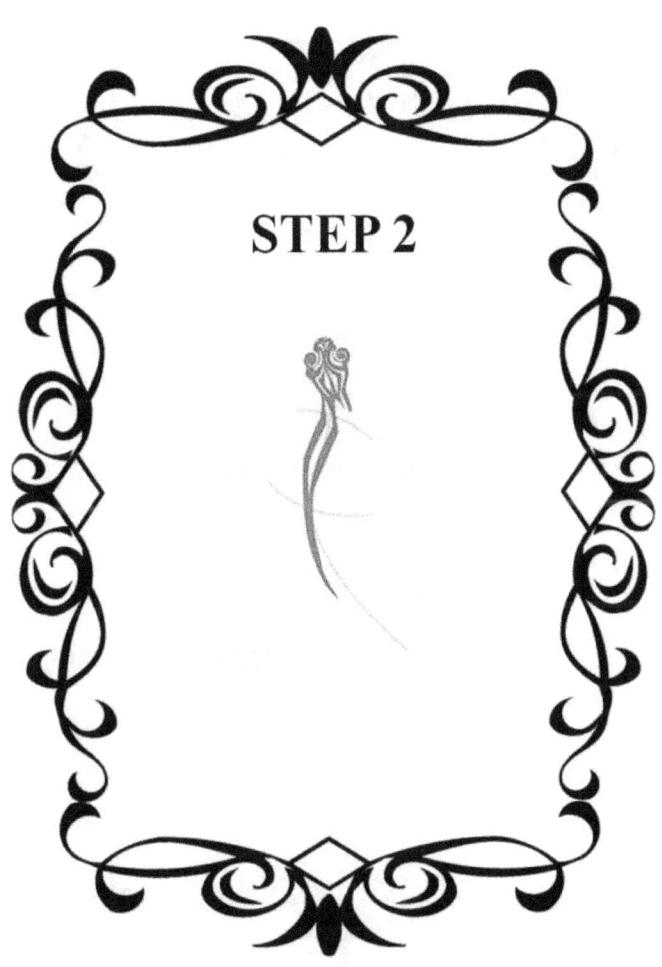

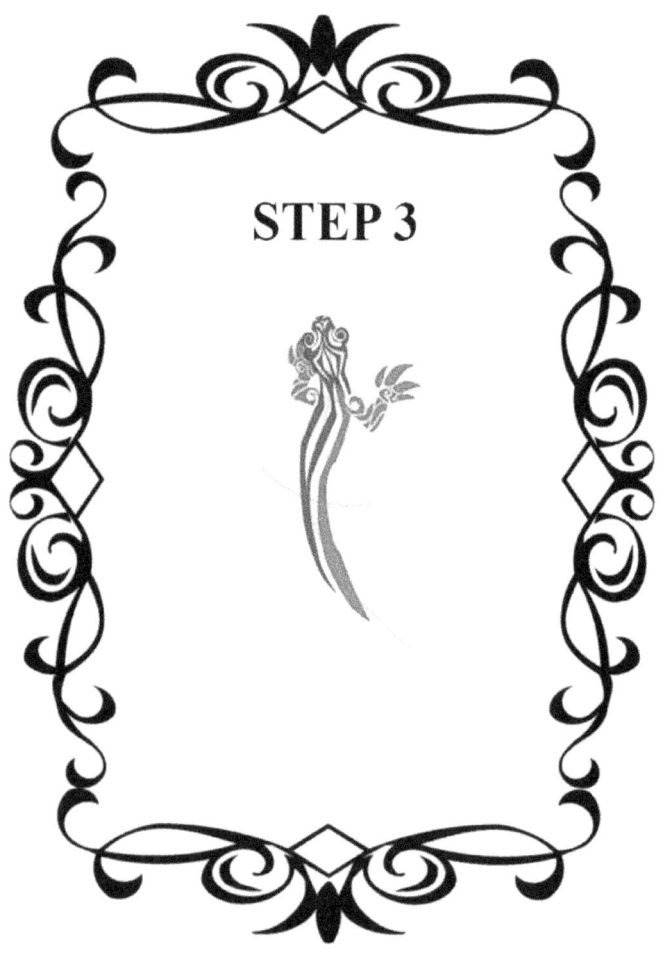

STEP 3

STEP 4

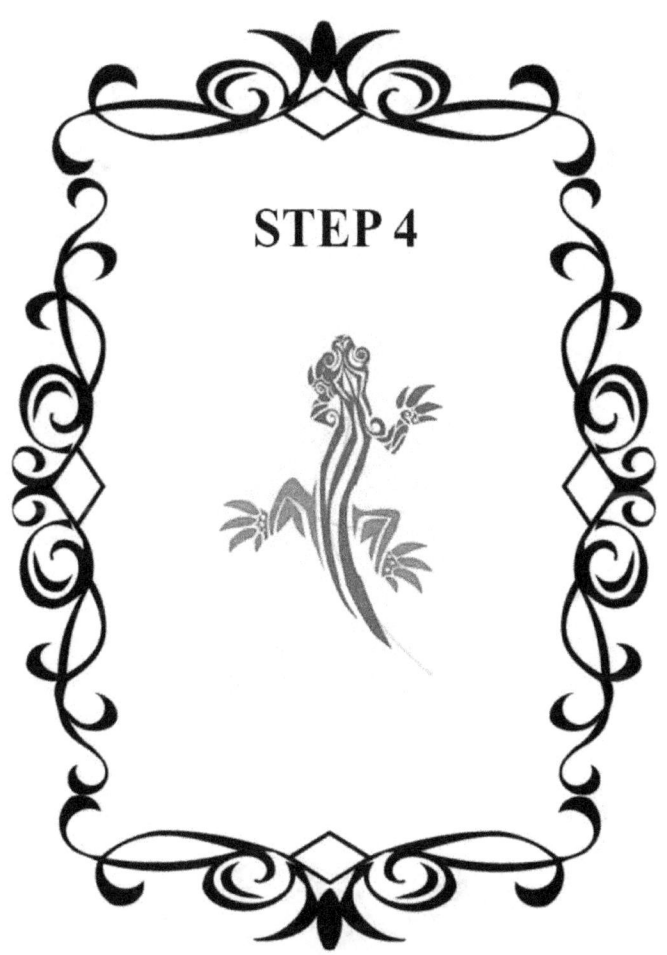

STEP 5

OCTOPUS TATTOO

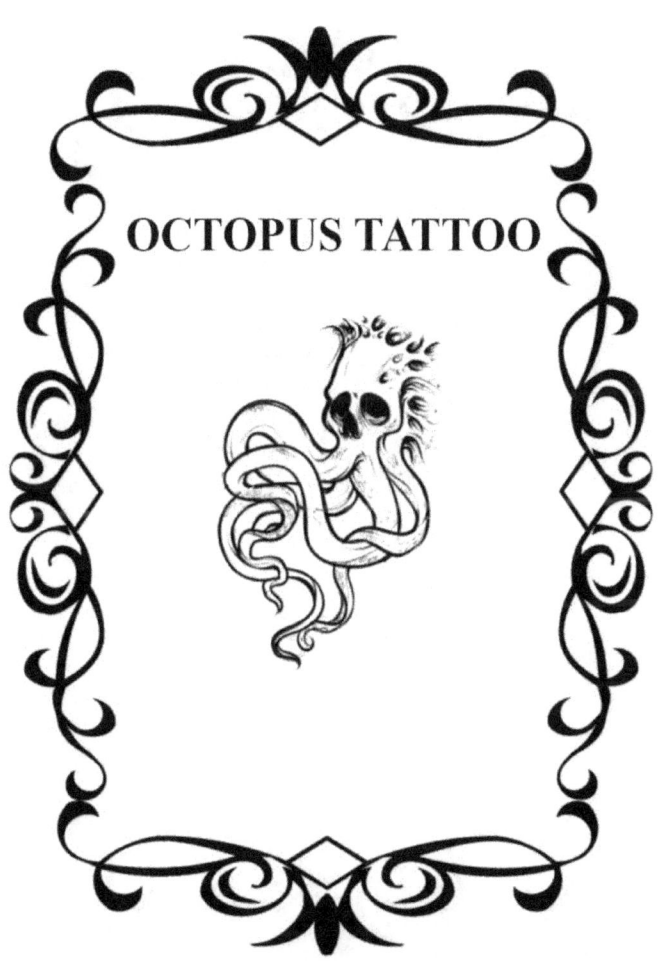

STEP 1

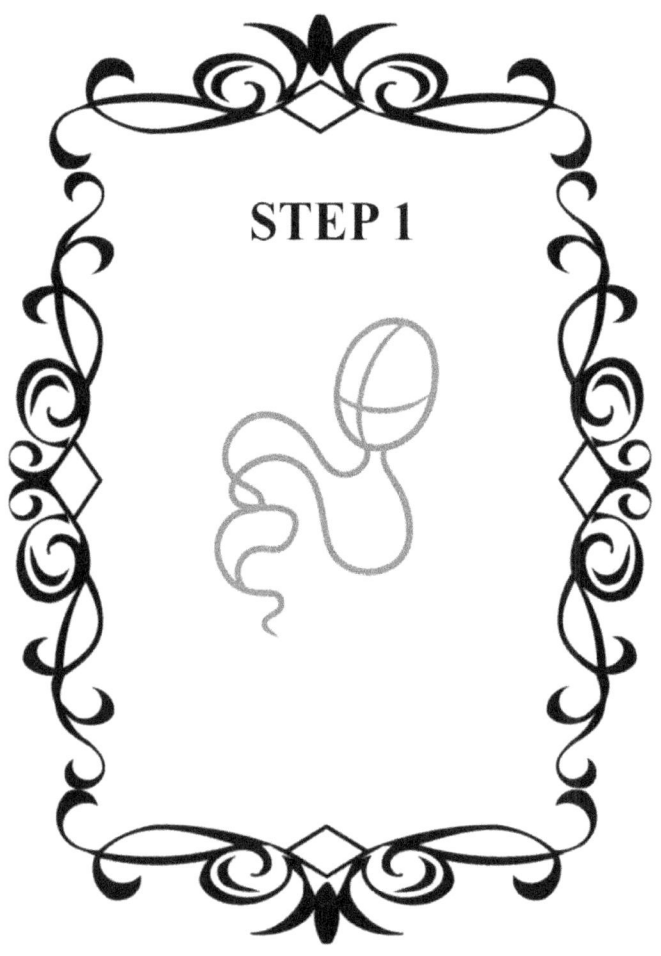

STEP 2

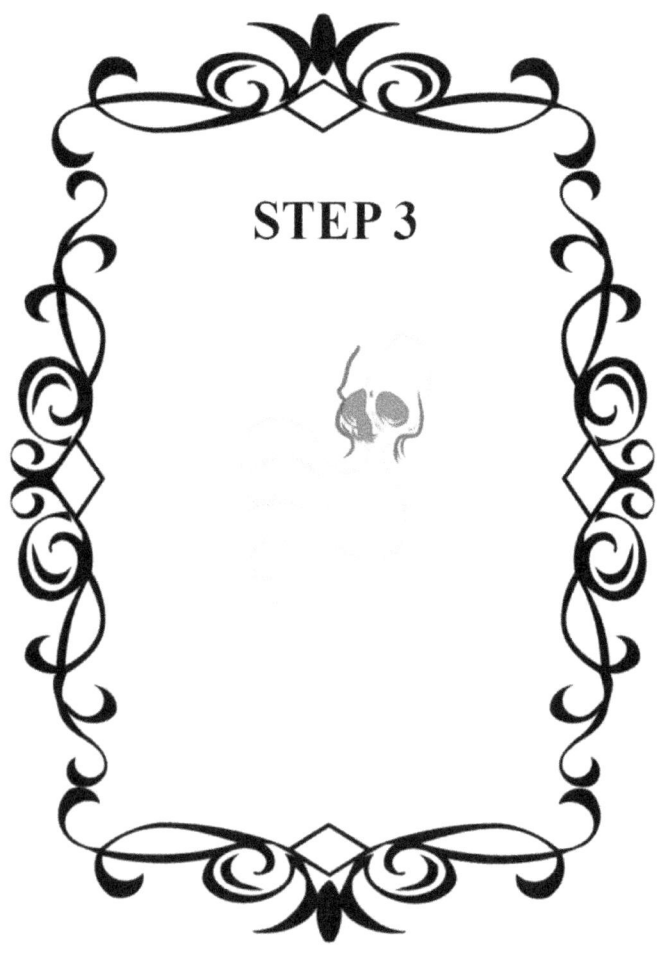

STEP 3

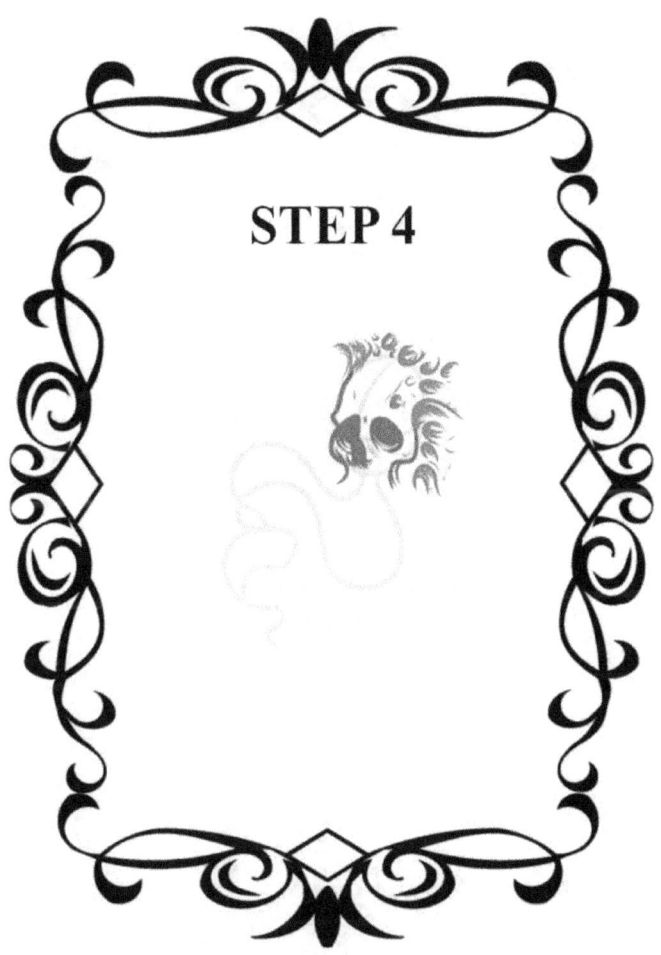

STEP 4

STEP 5

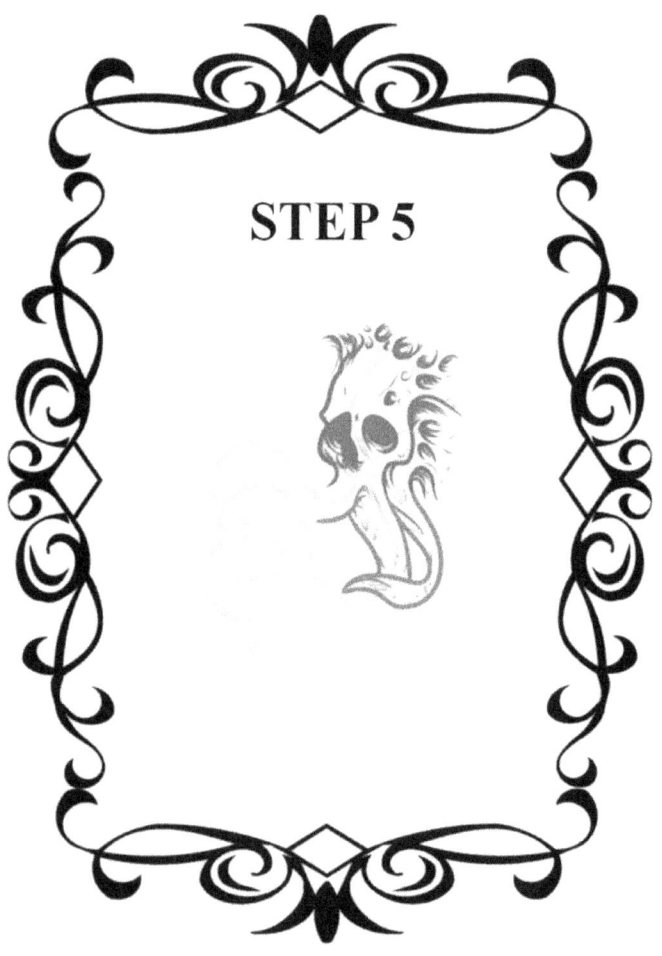

STEP 6

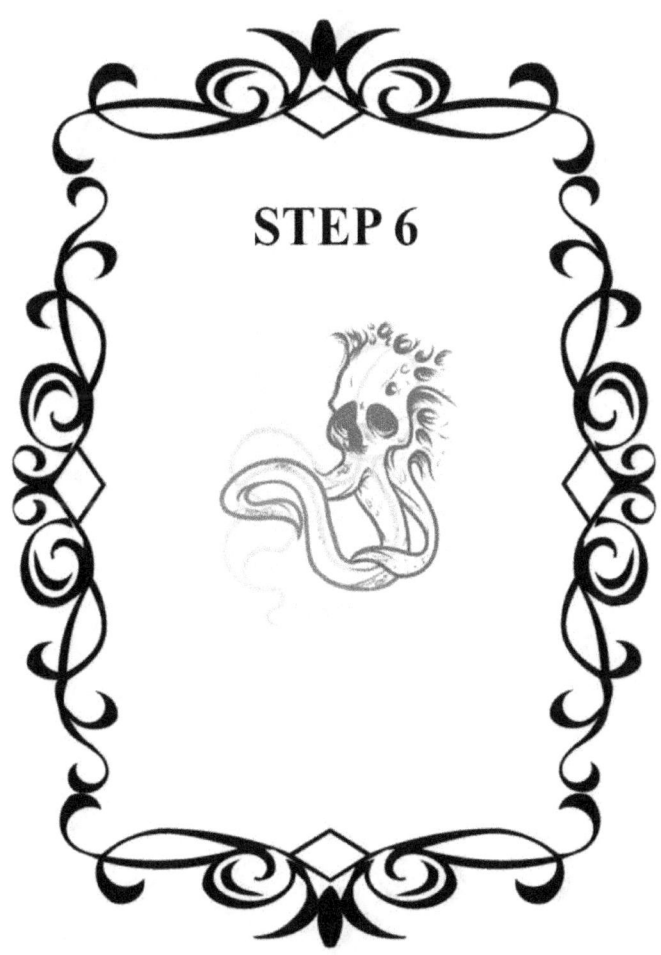

STEP 7

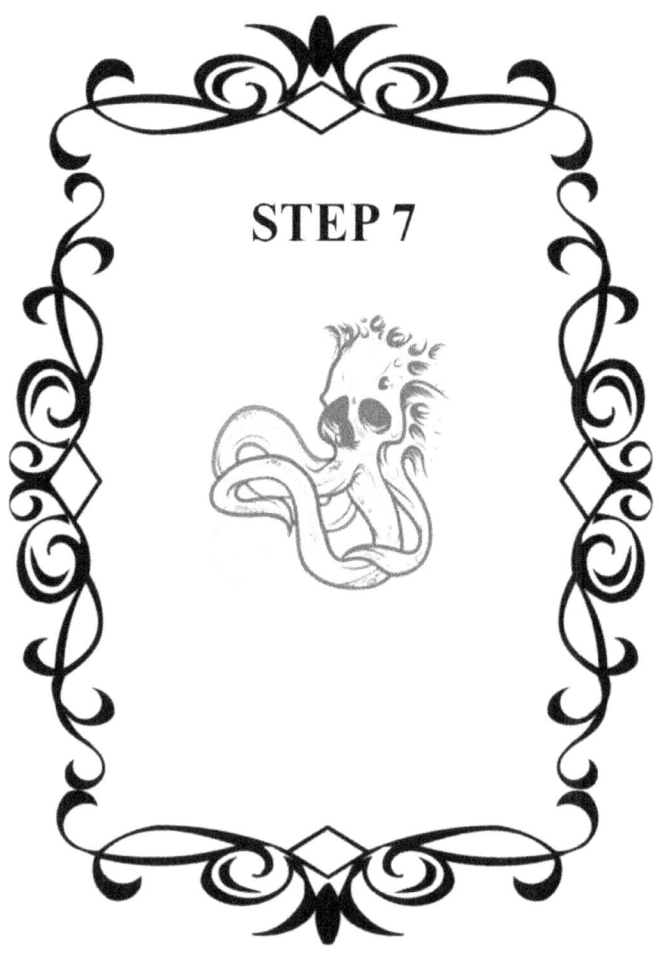

STEP 8

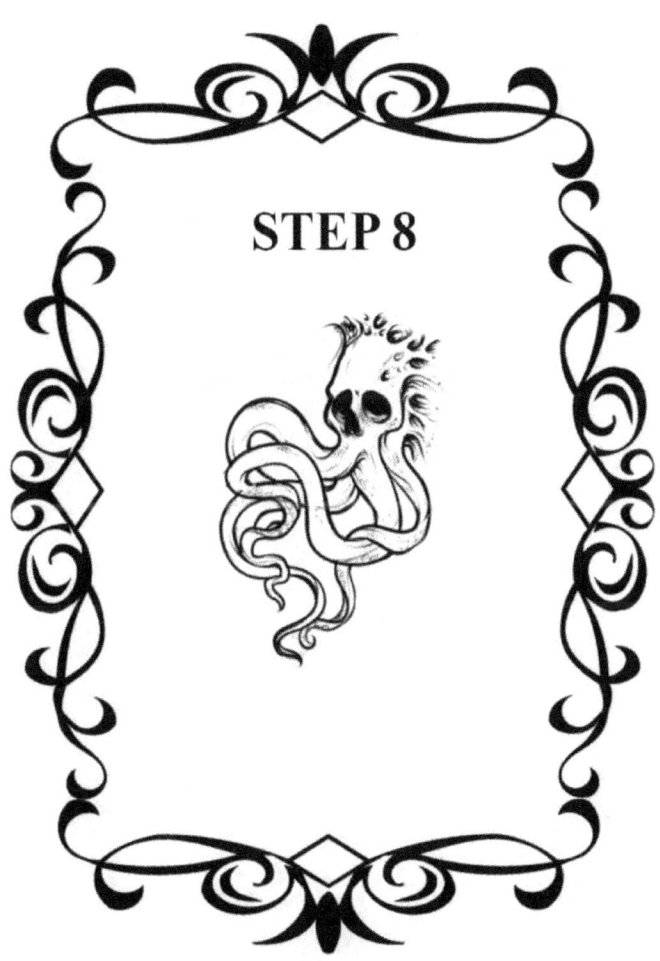

OWL TATTOO

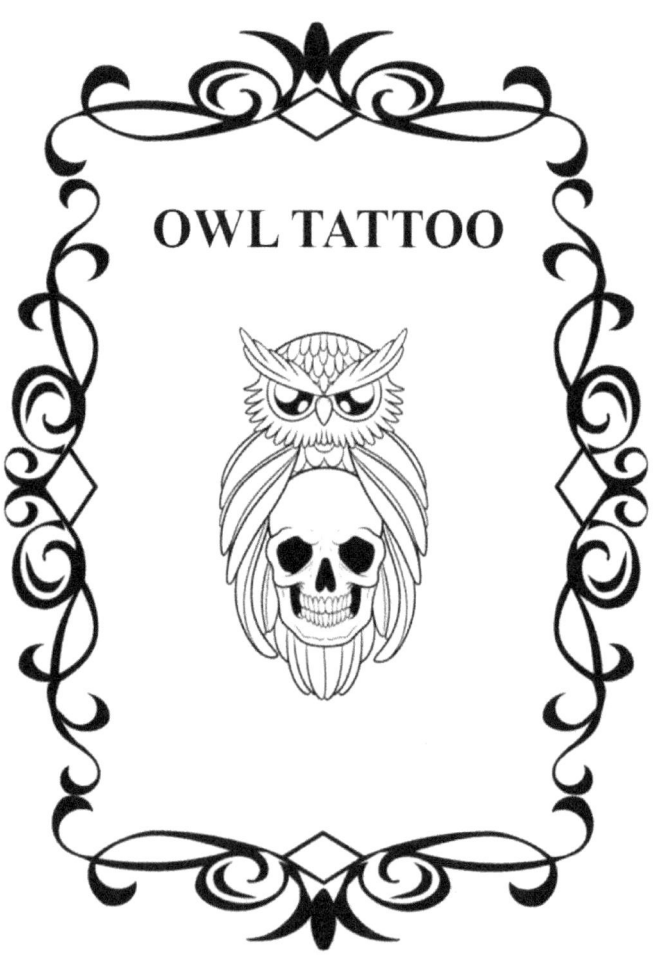

STEP 1

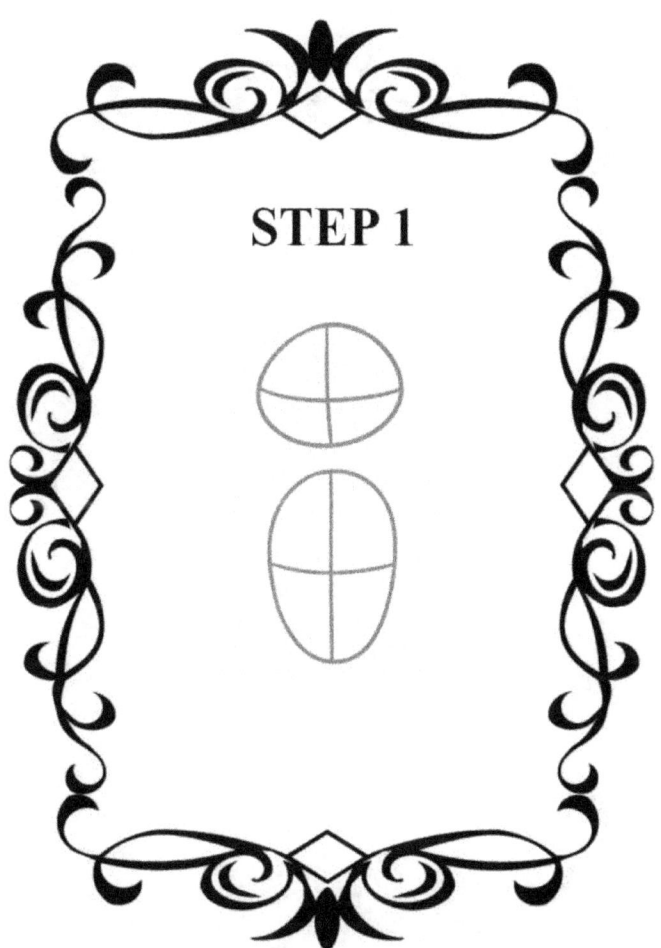

STEP 2

STEP 3

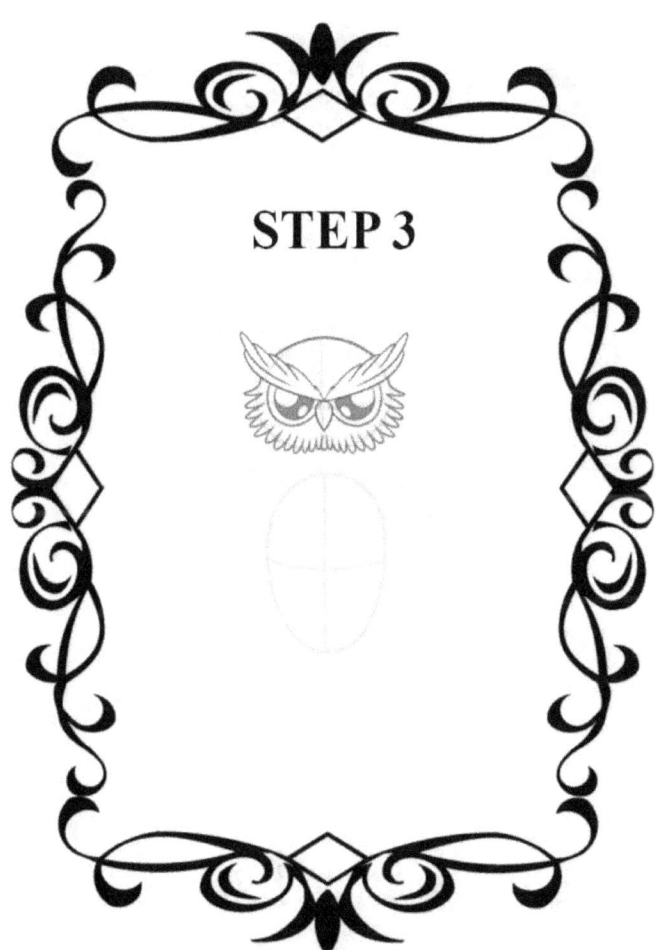

STEP 4

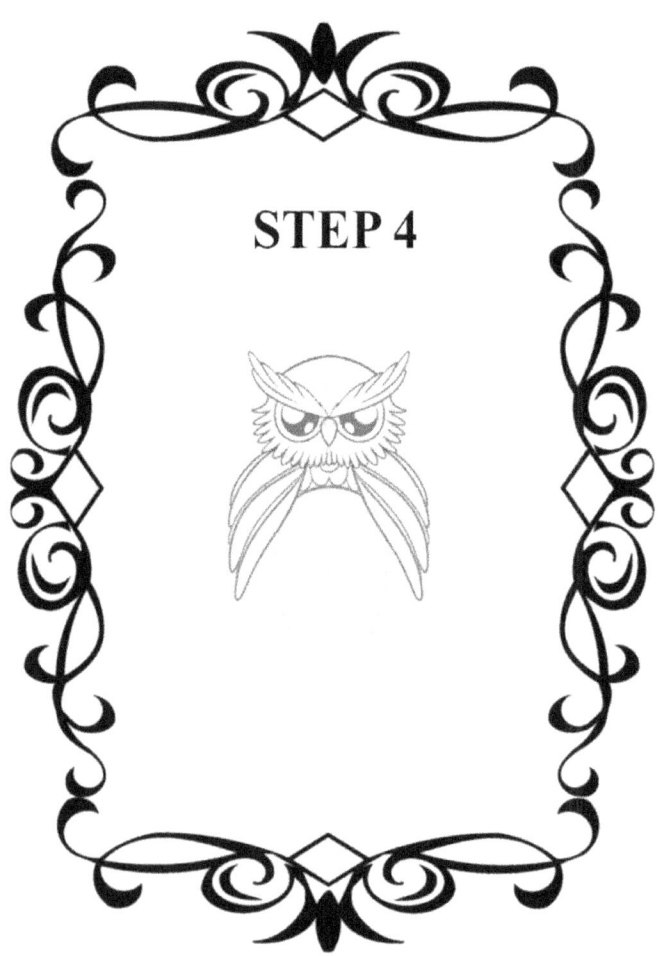

STEP 5

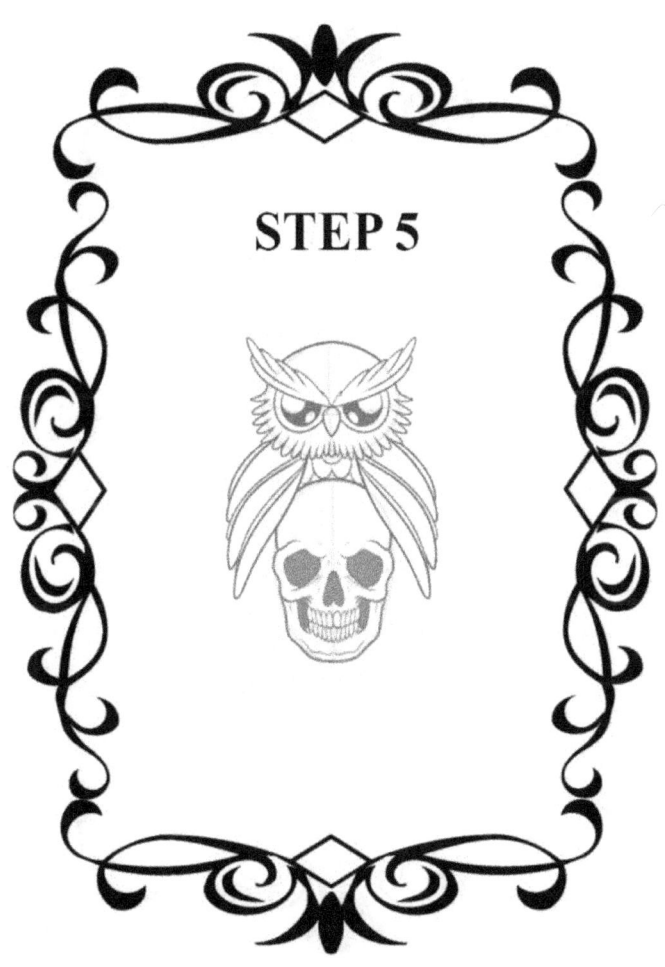

STEP 6

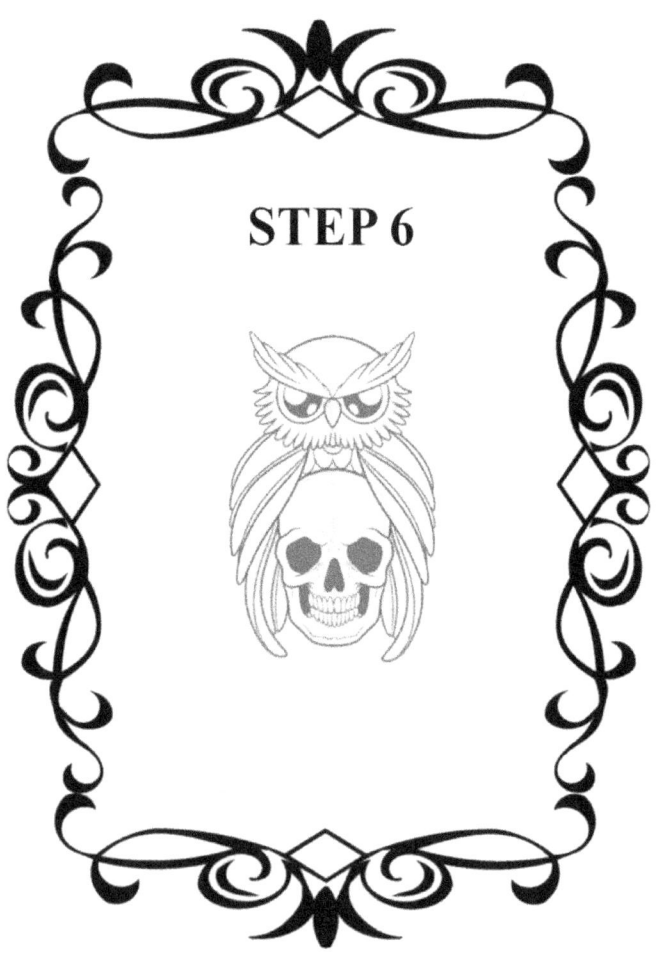

STEP 7

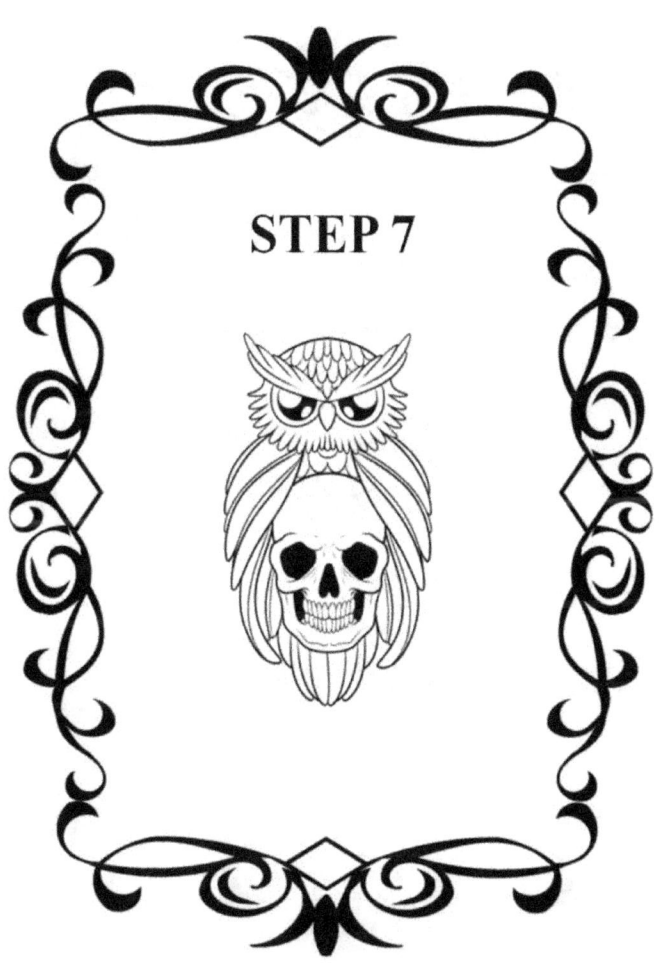

PANTHER TATTOO

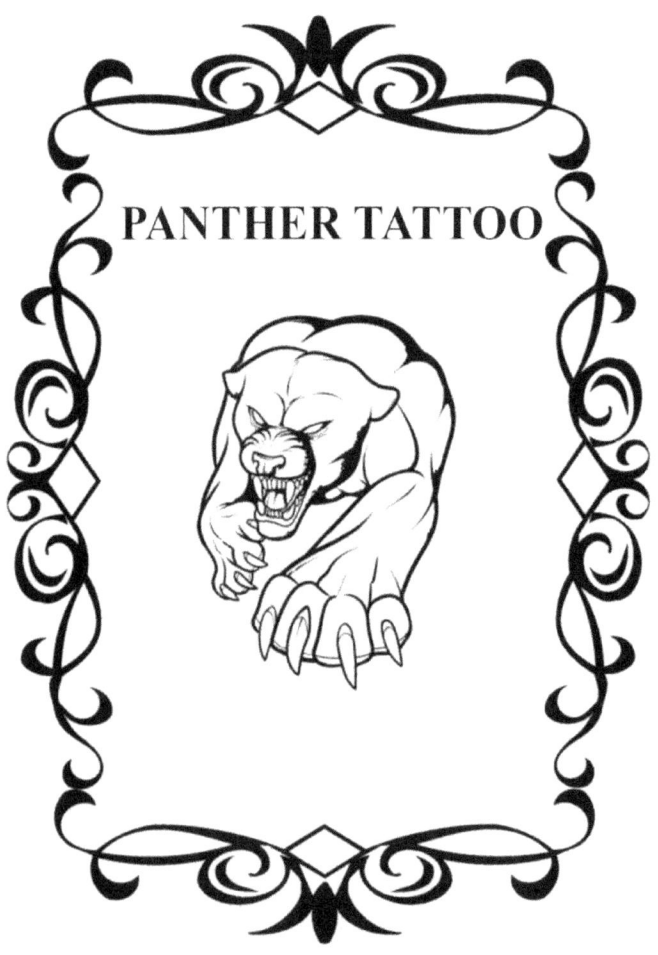

STEP 1

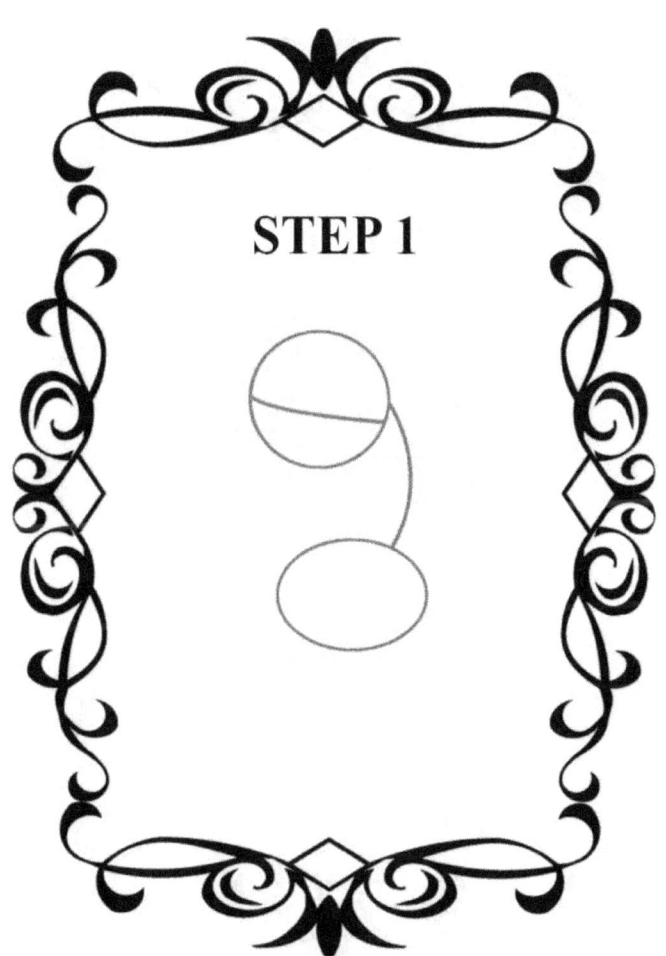

STEP 2

STEP 3

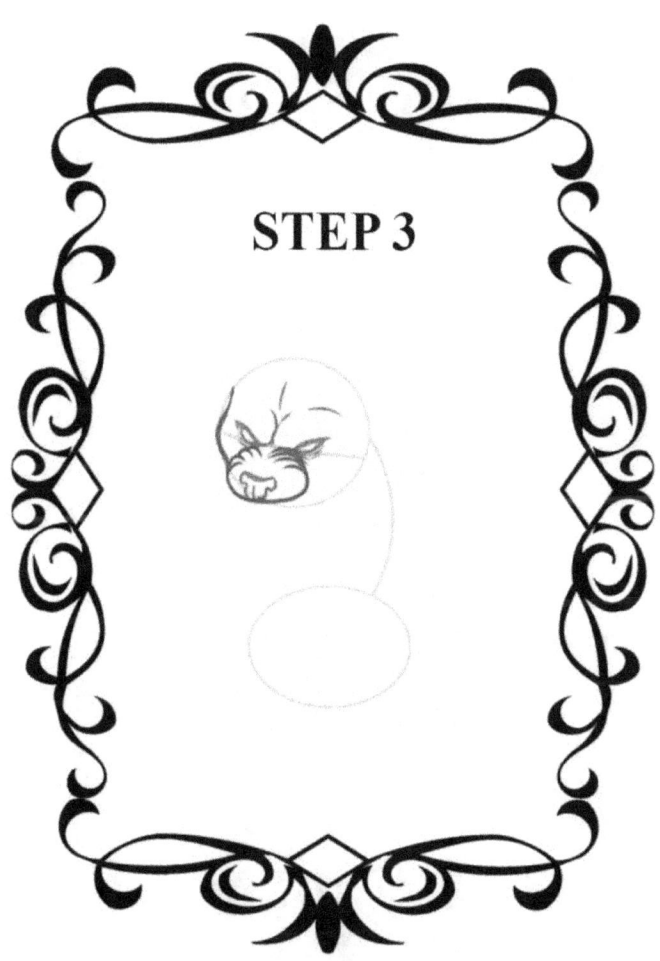

STEP 4

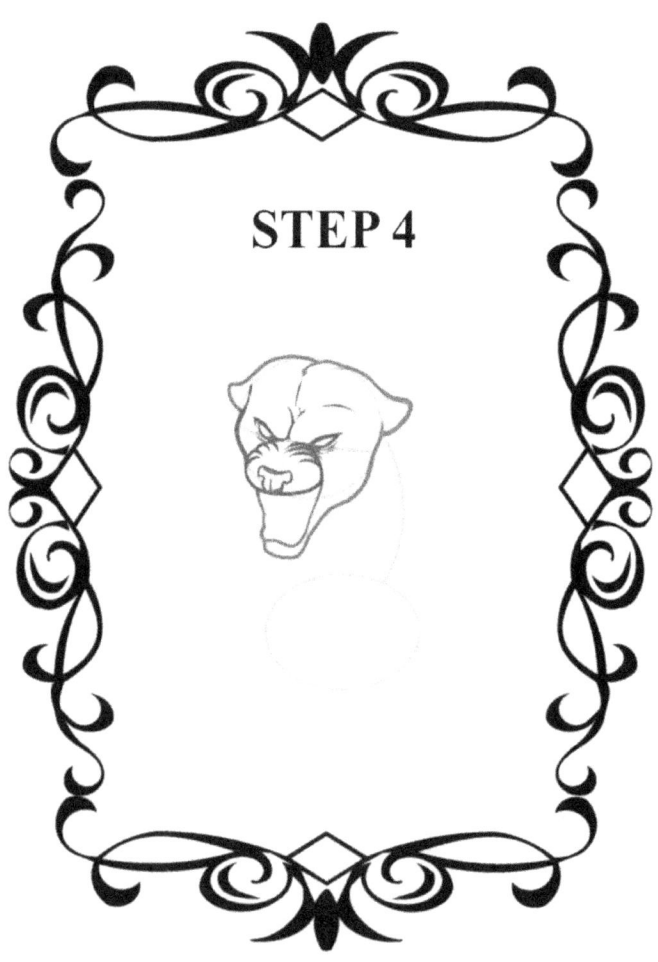

STEP 5

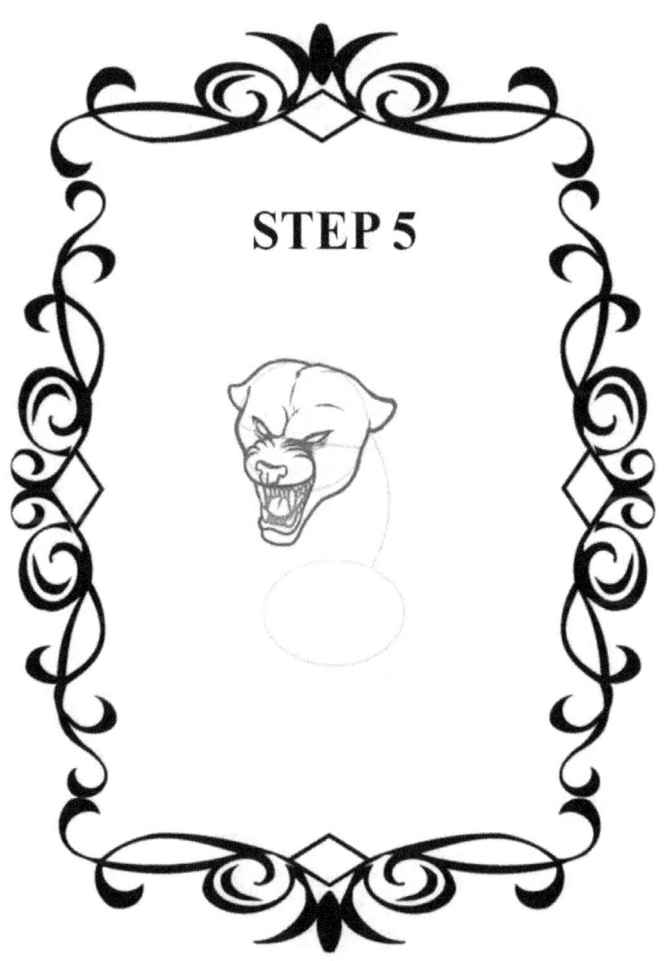

STEP 6

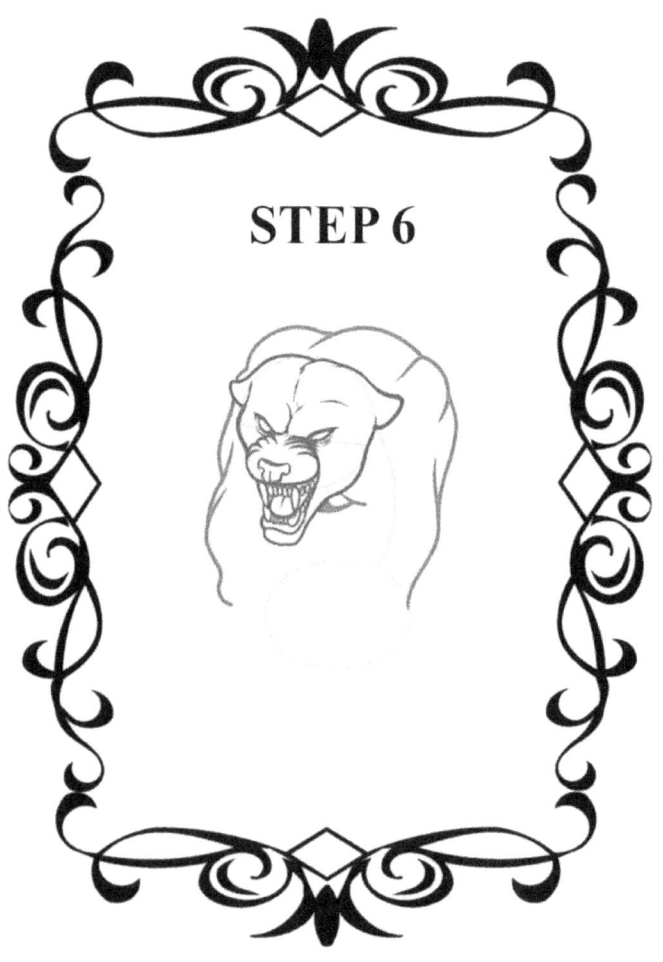

STEP 7

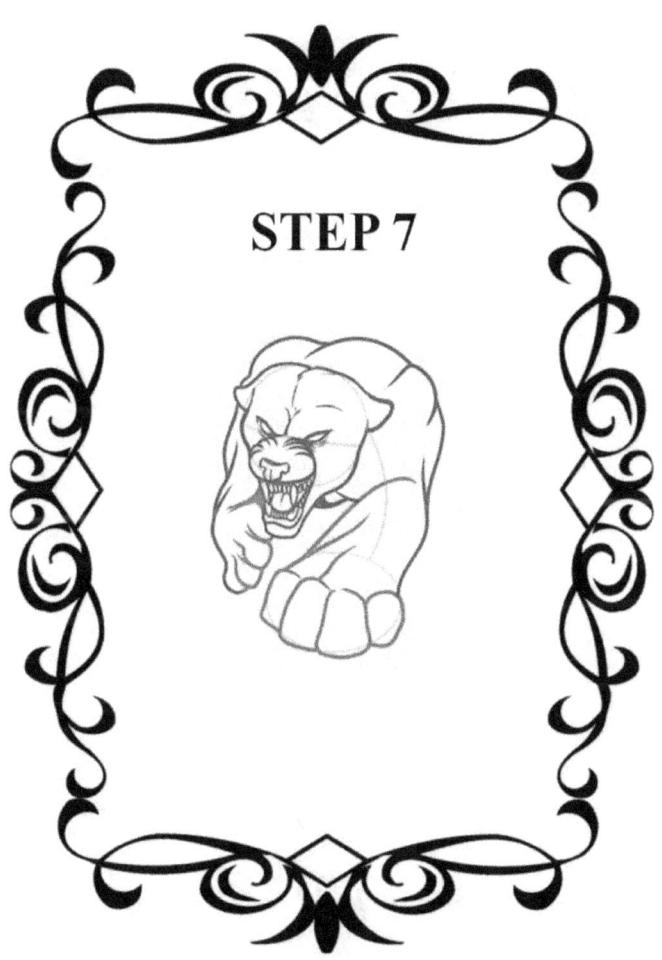

STEP 8

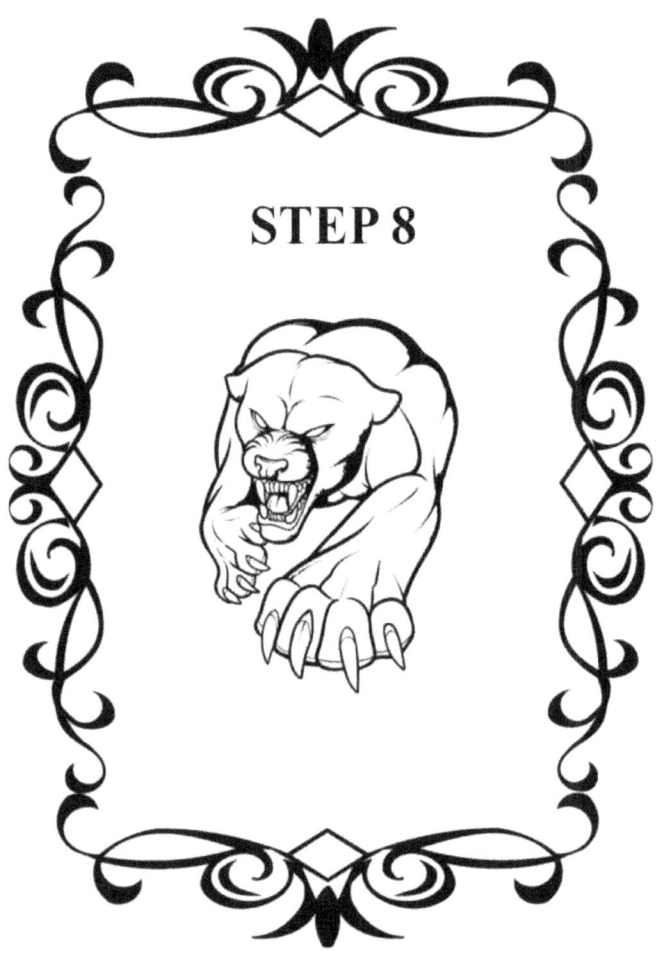

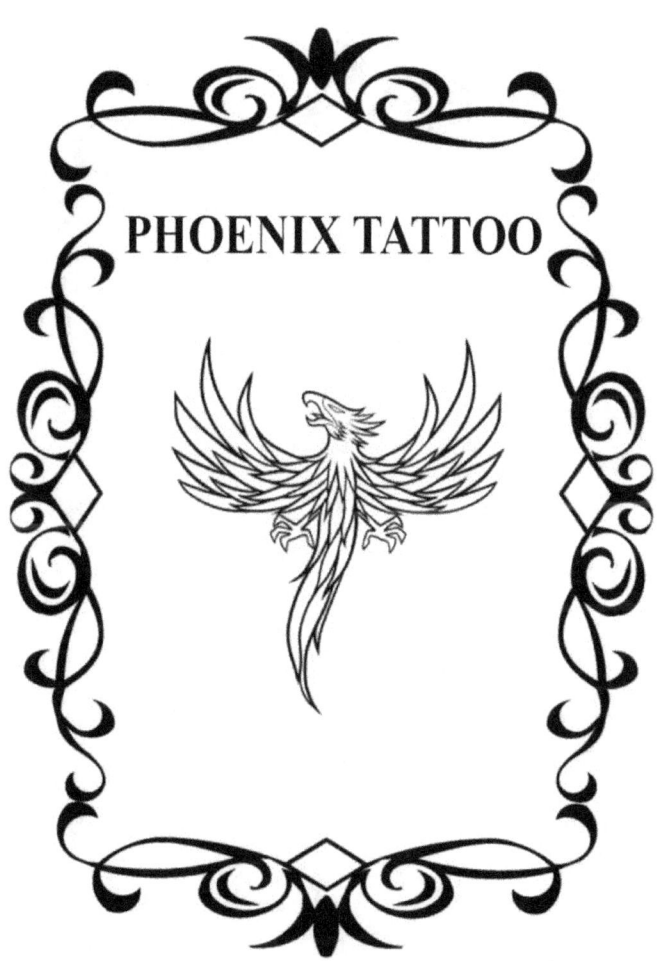

PHOENIX TATTOO

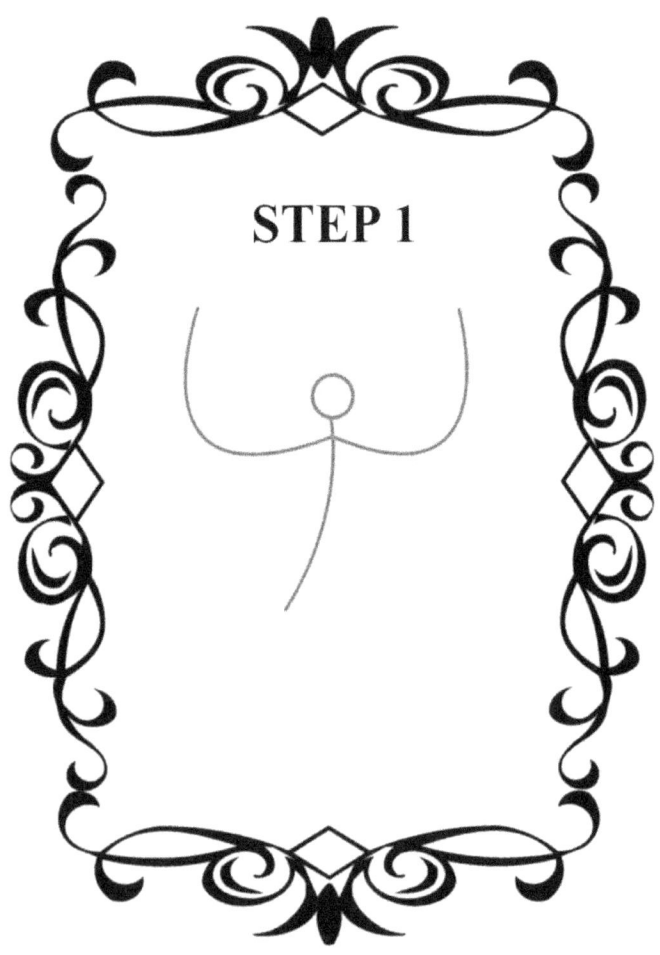

STEP 1

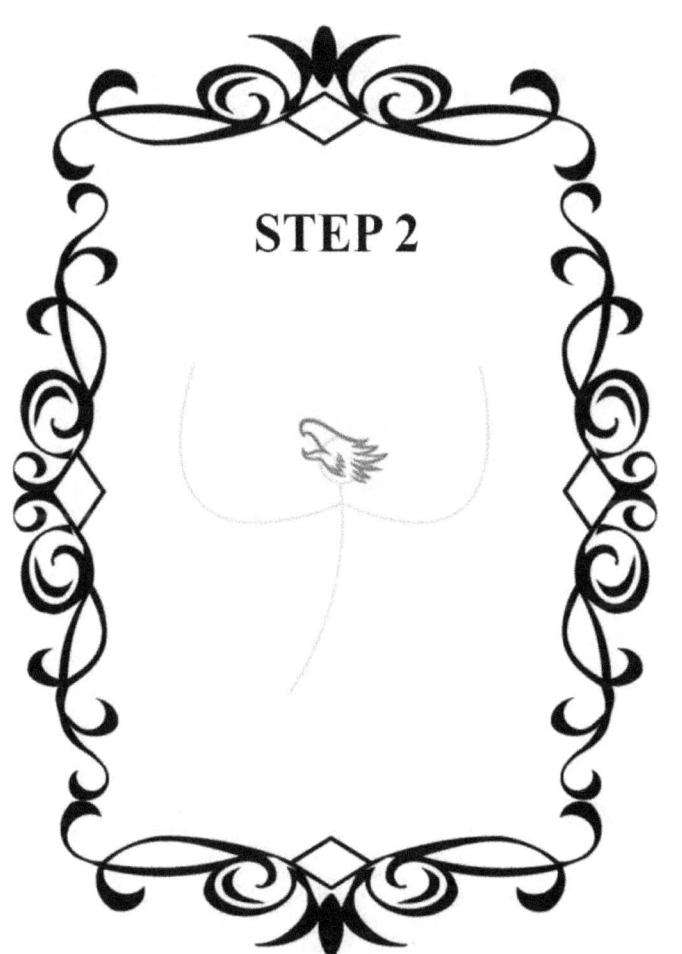

STEP 2

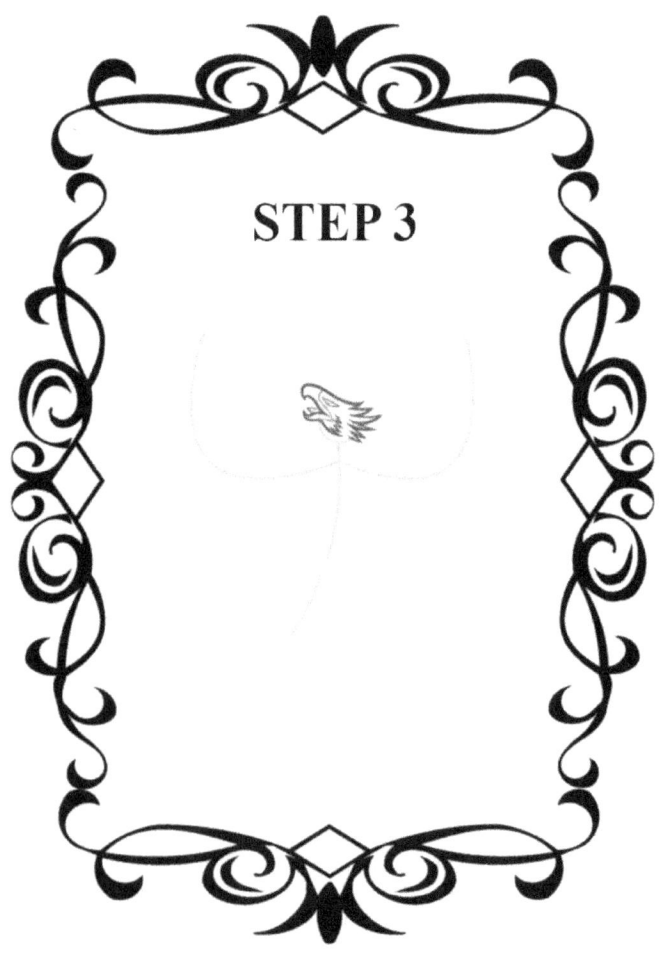

STEP 3

STEP 4

STEP 5

STEP 6

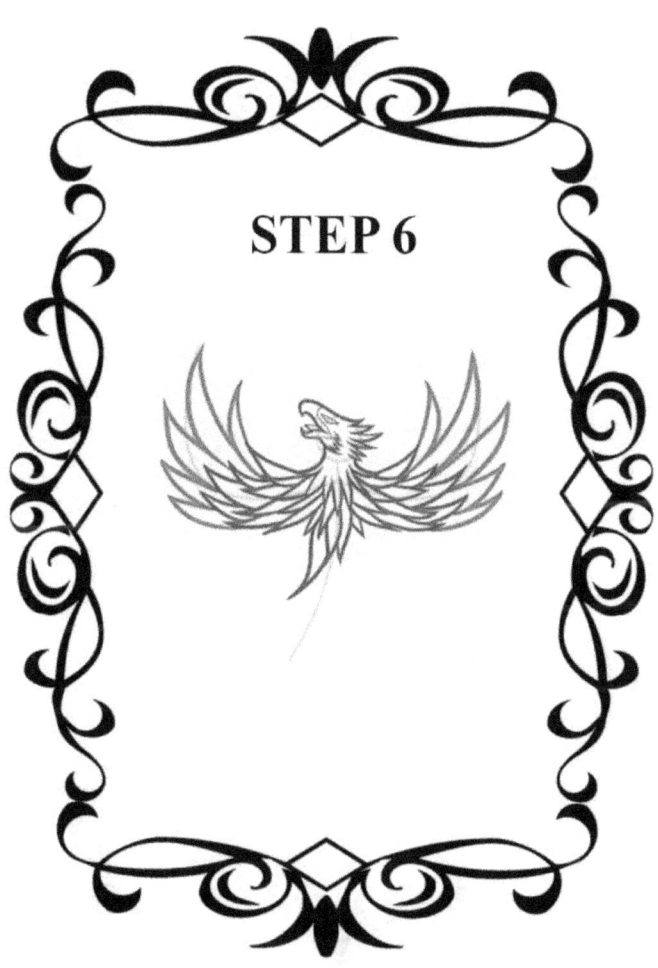

STEP 7

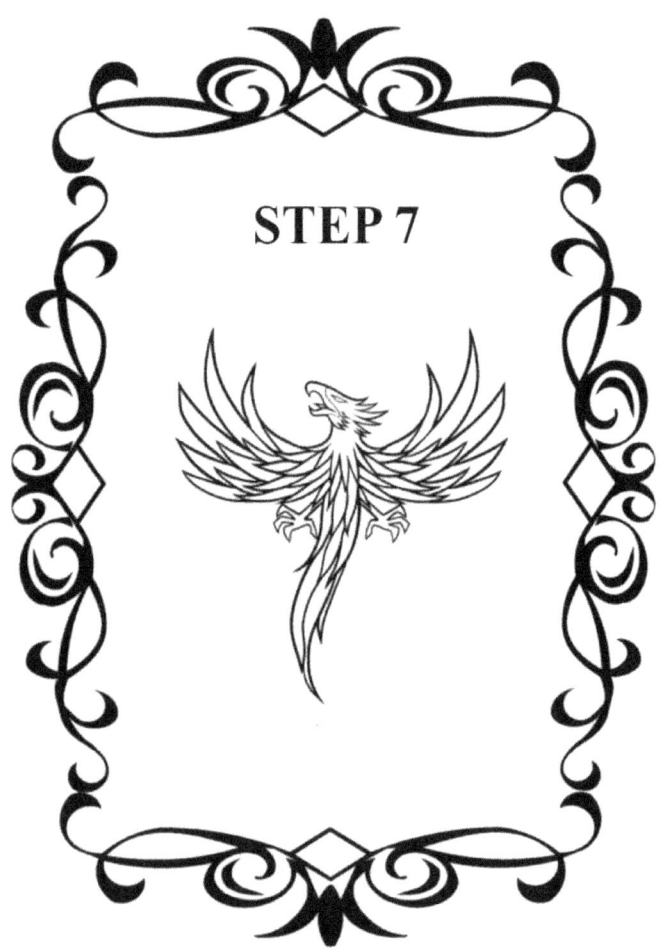

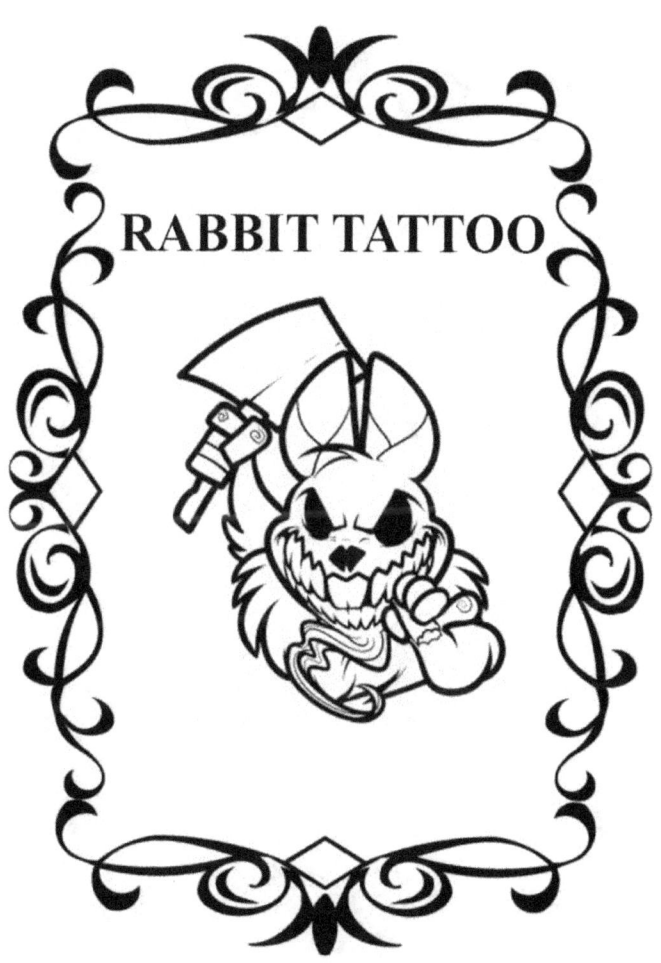

RABBIT TATTOO

STEP 1

STEP 2

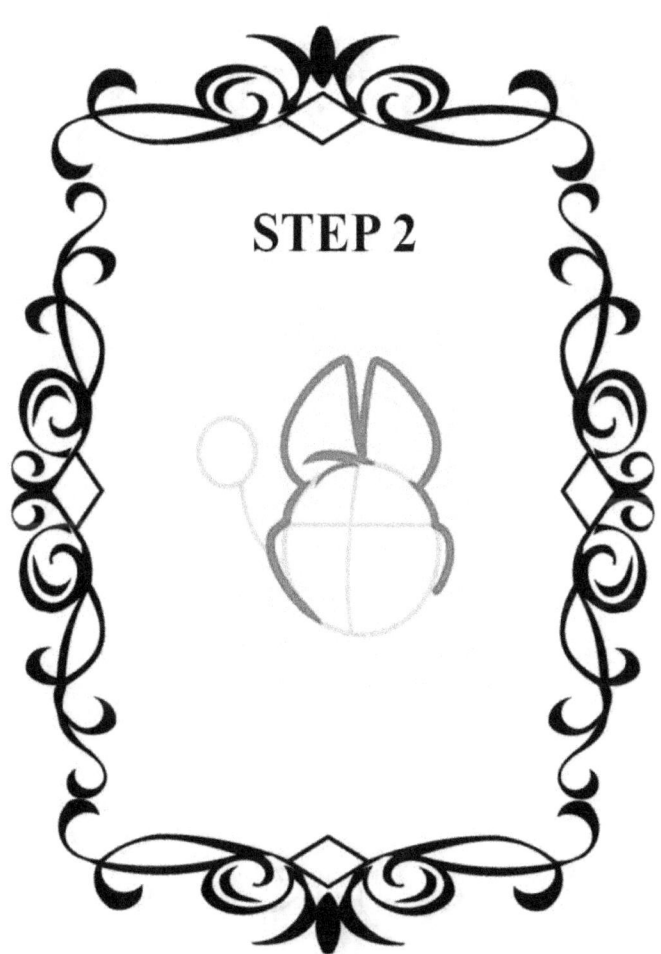

74

STEP 3

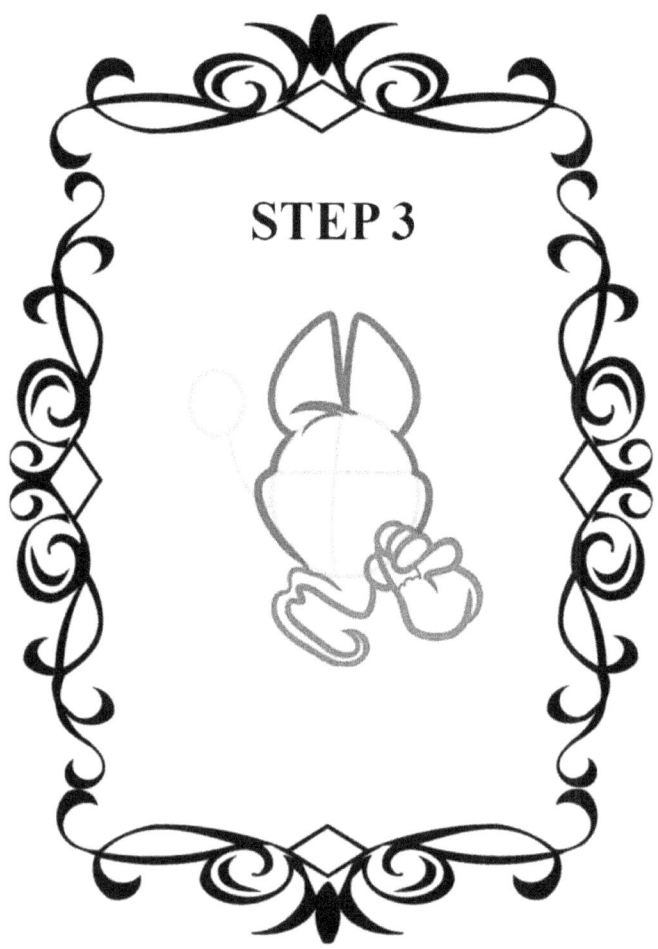

STEP 4

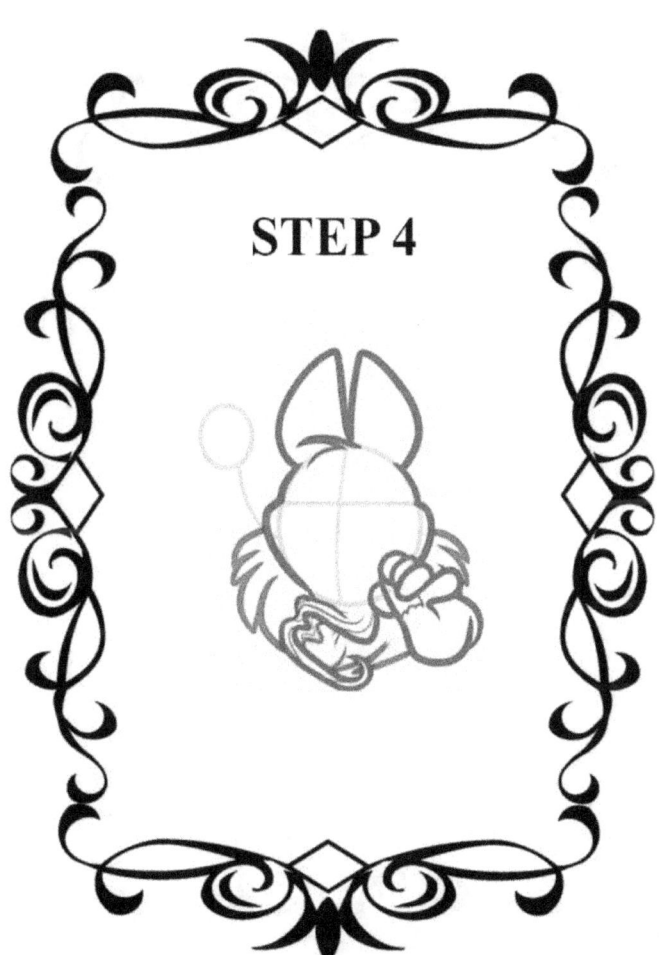

STEP 5

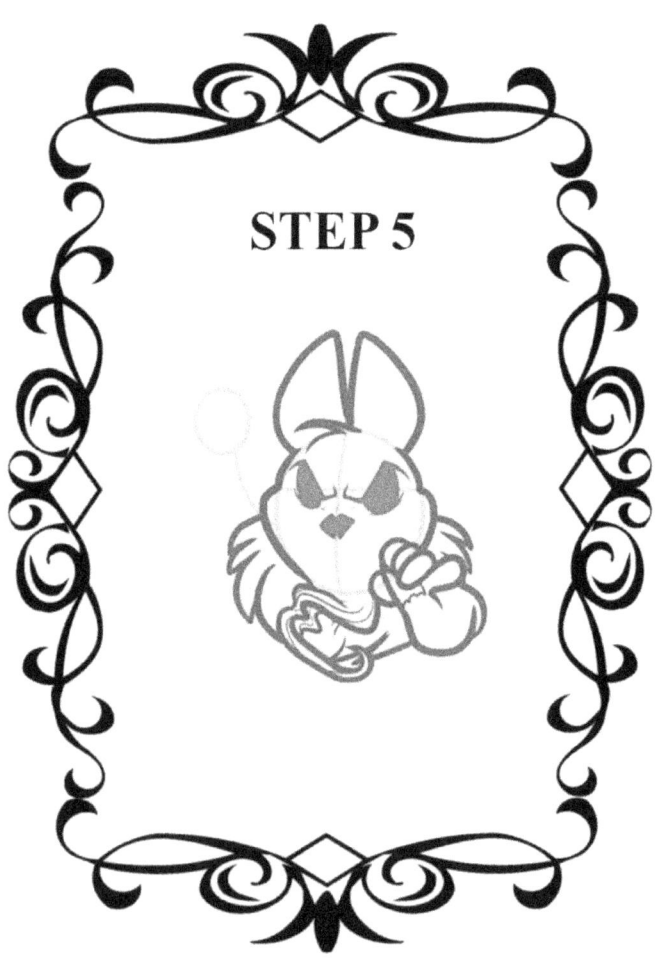

STEP 6

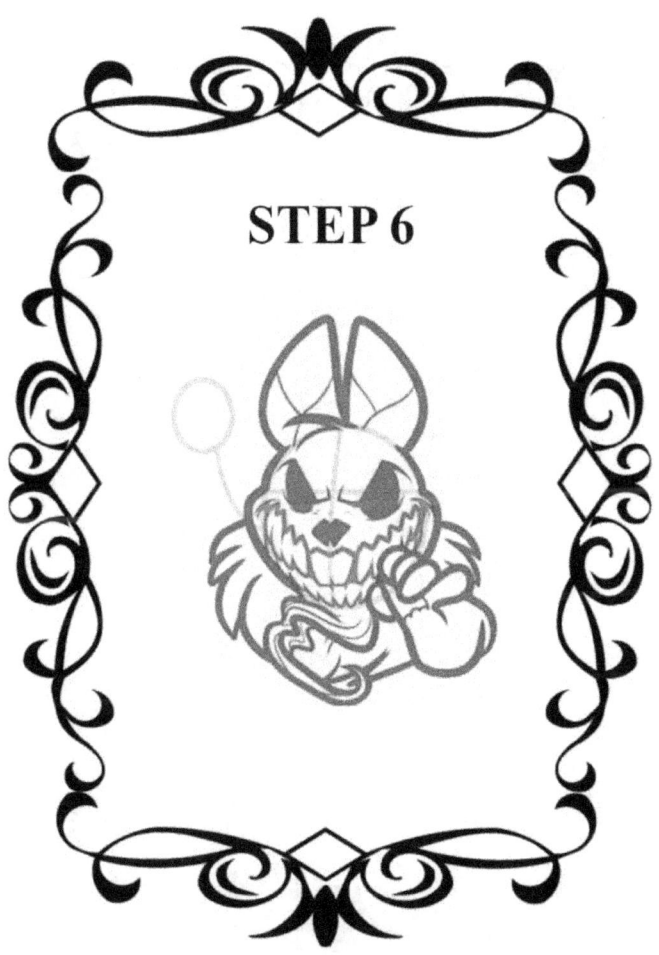

STEP 7

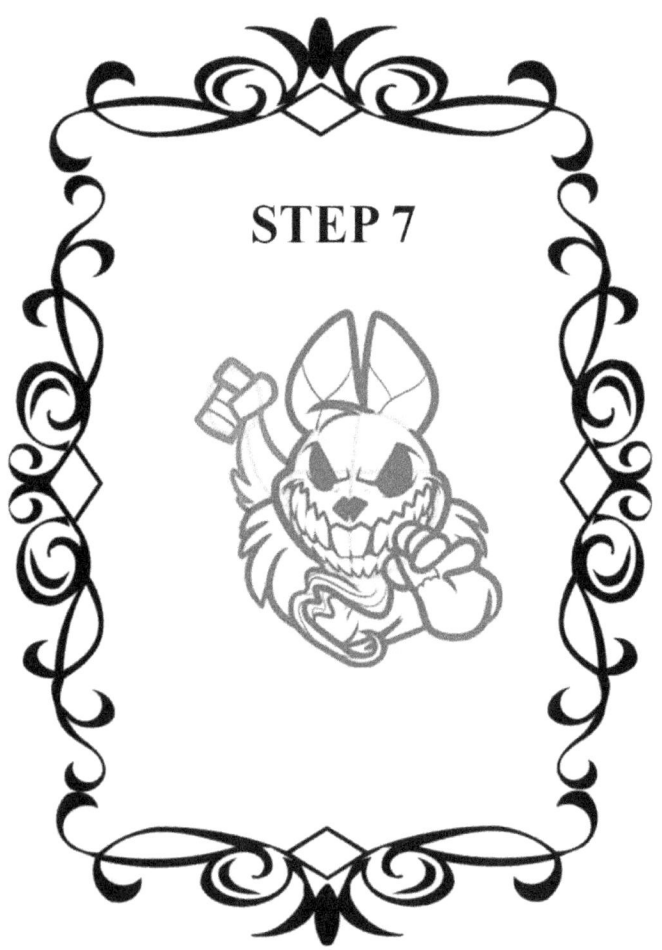

STEP 8

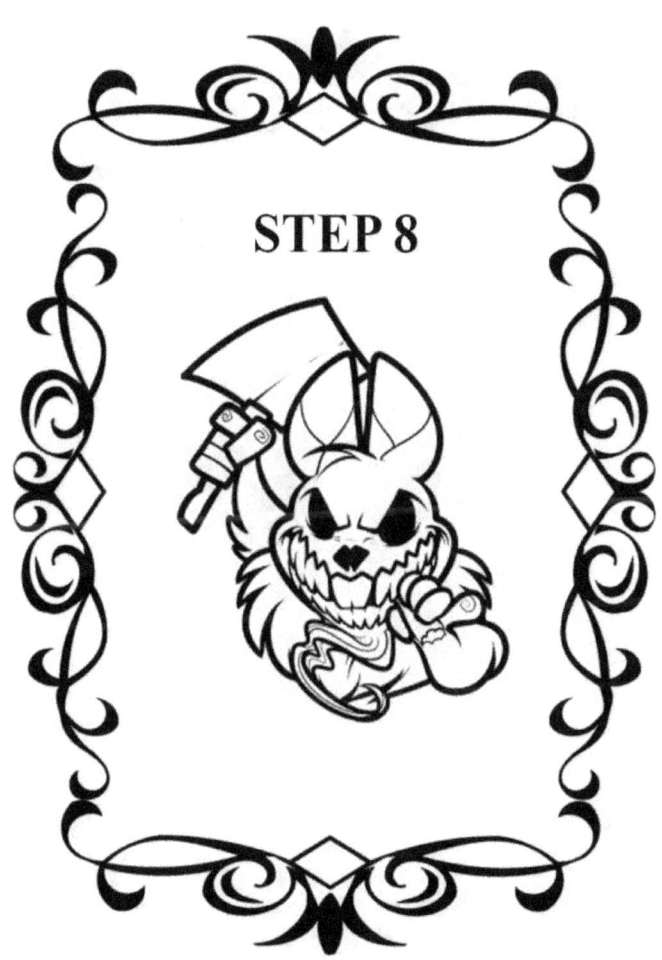

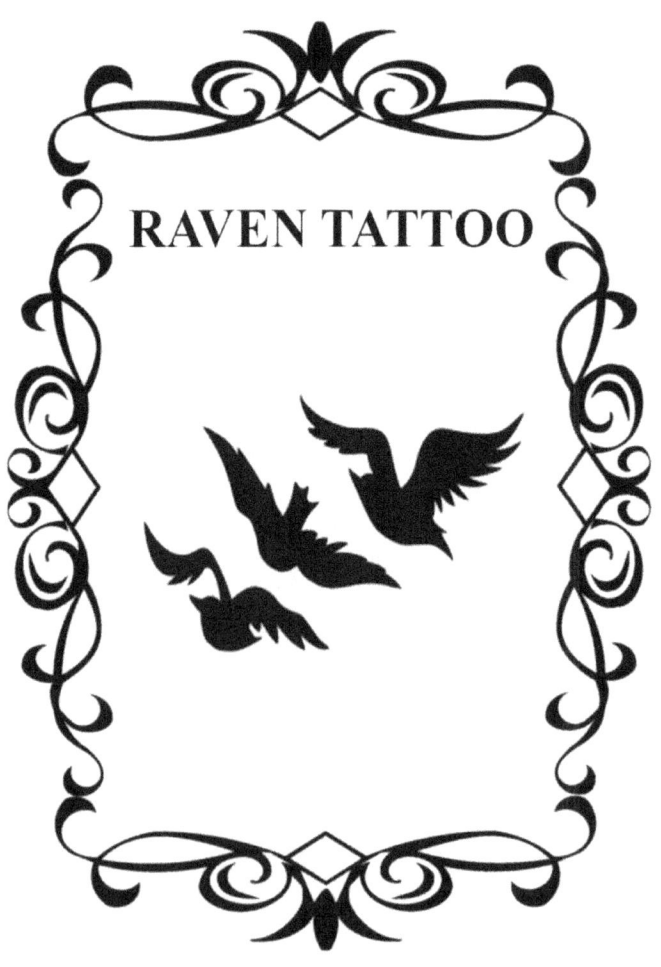

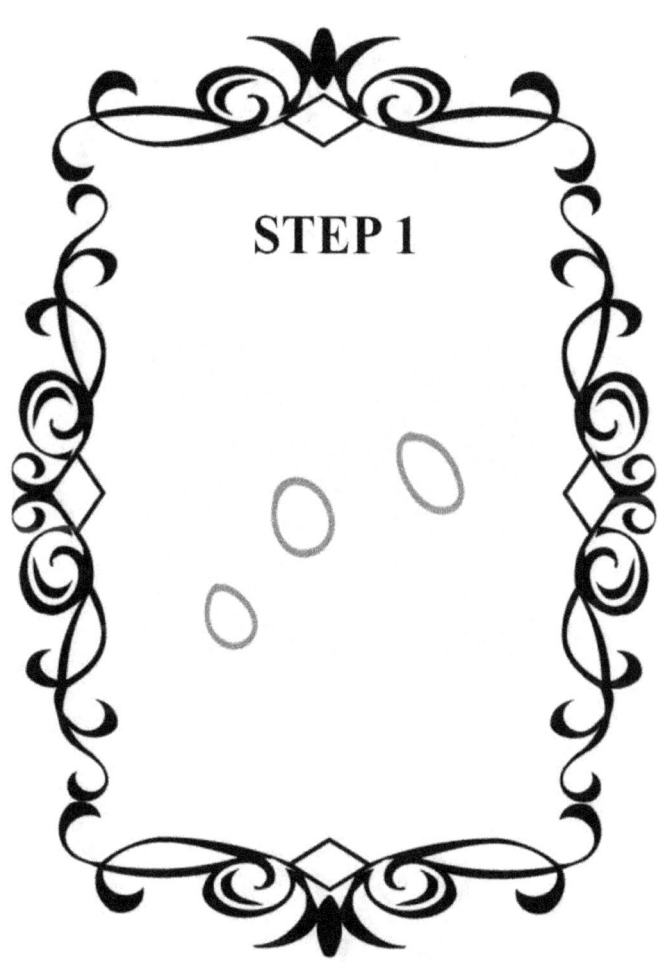

STEP 1

STEP 2

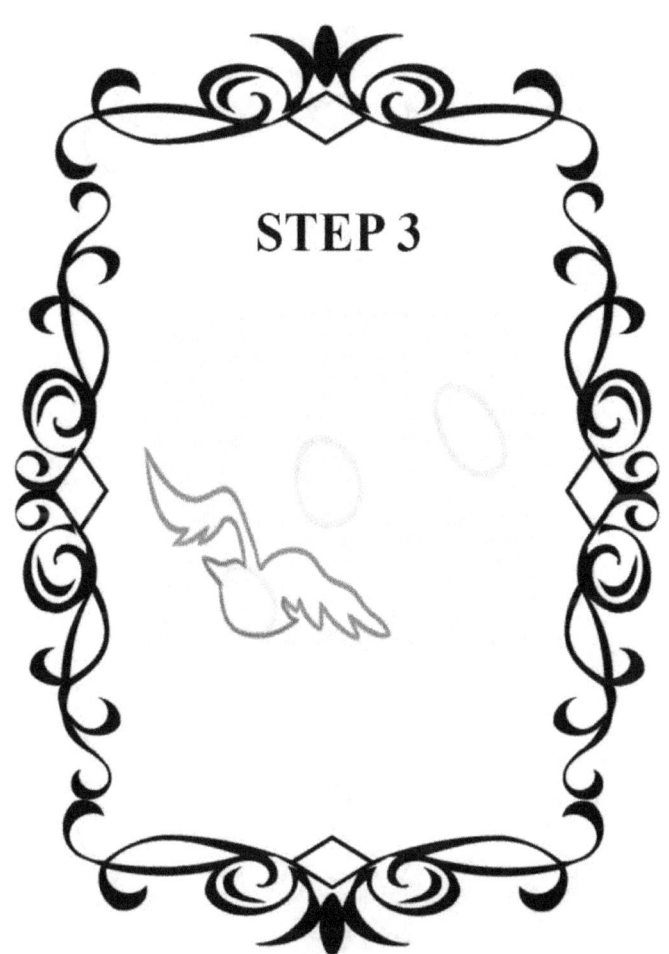

STEP 3

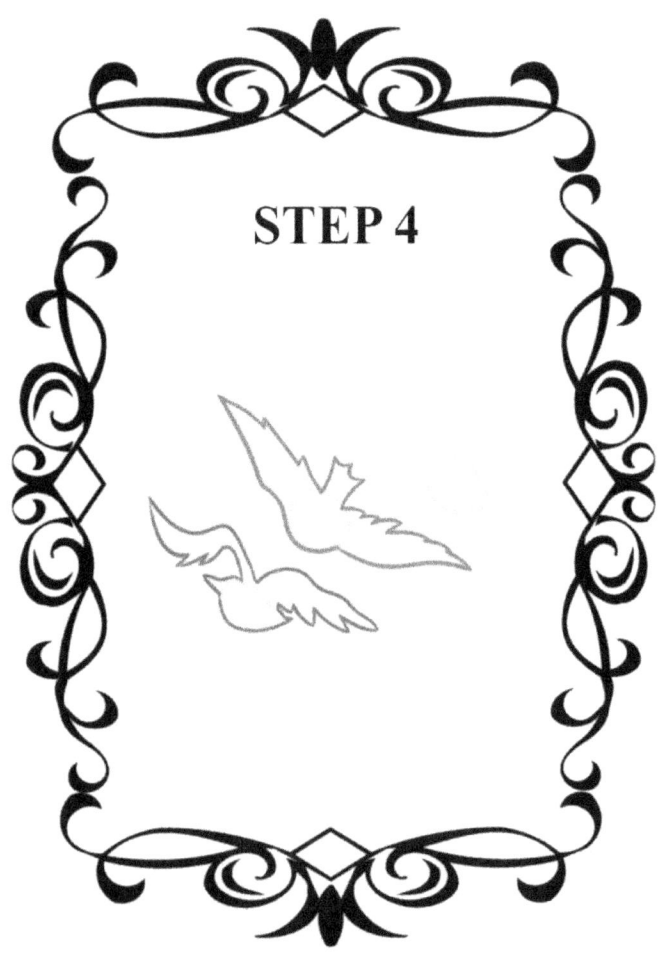

STEP 4

STEP 5

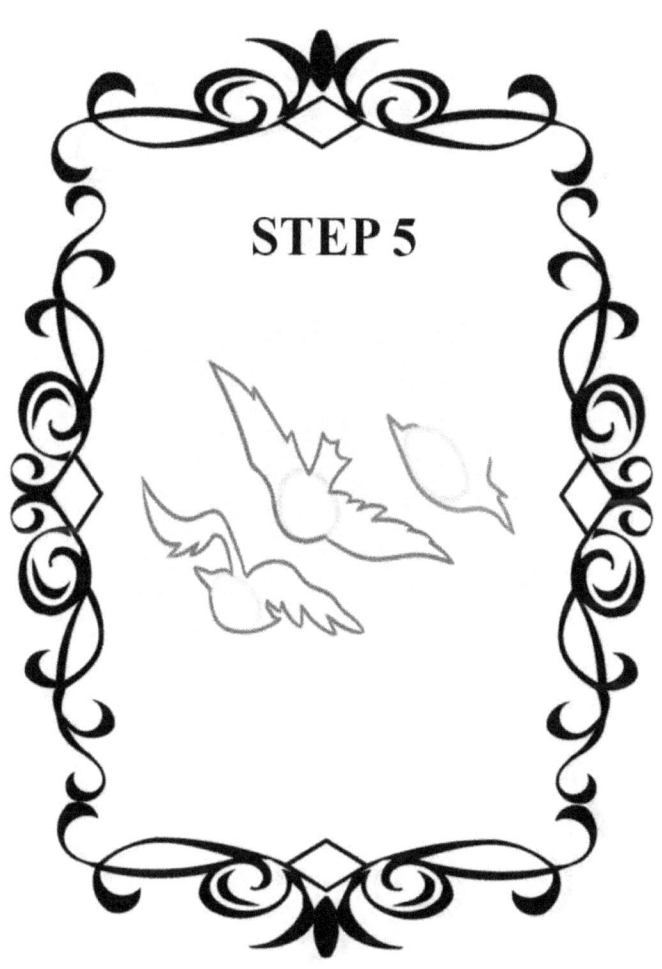

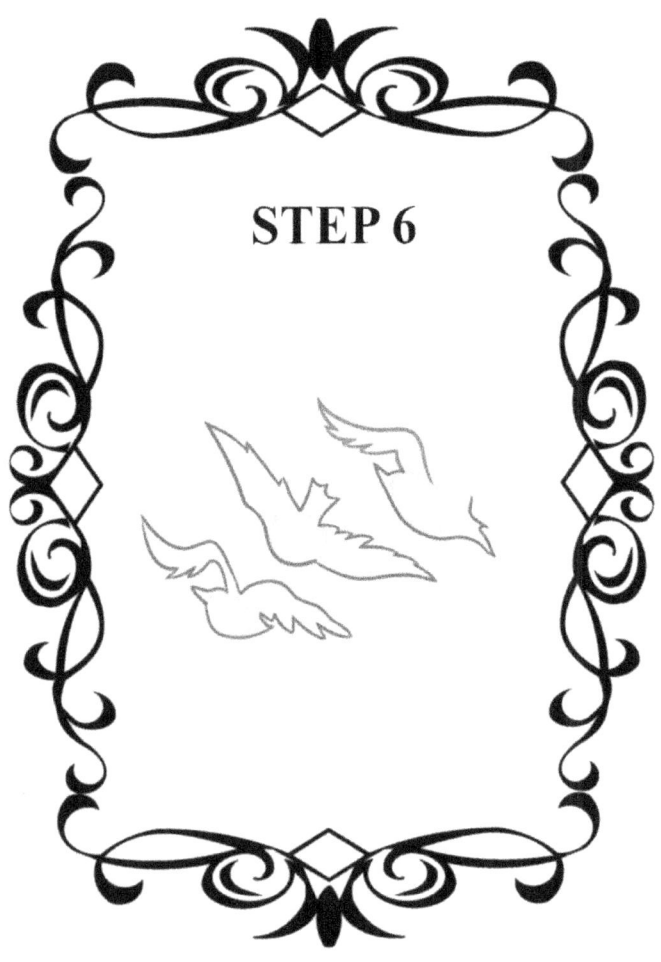

STEP 6

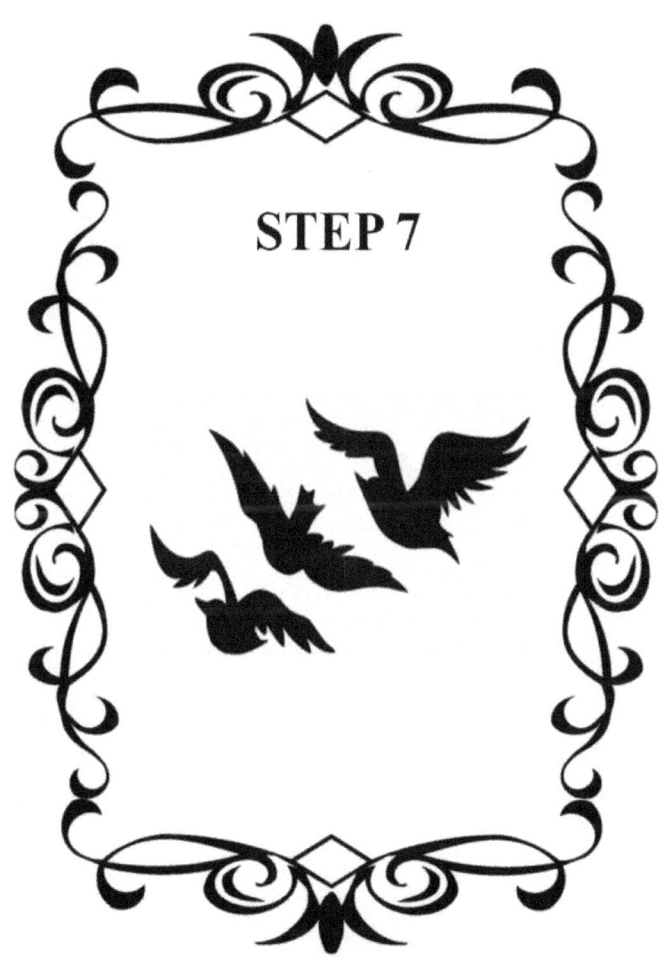

STEP 7

www.ingramcontent.com/pod-product-compliance
Lightning Source LLC
Chambersburg PA
CBHW071606170526
45166CB00003B/1007